Love
ILLUMINATED

Love
ILLUMINATED

Exploring Life's Most Mystifying Subject
(with the Help of 50,000 Strangers)

DANIEL JONES

wm

WILLIAM MORROW
An Imprint of HarperCollins*Publishers*

LOVE ILLUMINATED. Copyright © 2014 by Daniel Jones. All rights reserved. Printed in the United States of America. No part of this book may be used or reproduced in any manner whatsoever without written permission except in the case of brief quotations embodied in critical articles and reviews. For information address Harper-Collins Publishers, 10 East 53rd Street, New York, NY 10022.

HarperCollins books may be purchased for educational, business, or sales promotional use. For information please write the Special Markets Department at SPsales@harpercollins.com.

FIRST EDITION

Designed by Jamie Lynn Kerner

Library of Congress Cataloging-in-Publication Data has been applied for.

ISBN 978-0-06-221116-3

14 15 16 17 18   ov/rrd   10 9 8 7 6 5 4 3 2 1

For Charles and Vera Jones, my lifelong teachers
in the subject of love

CONTENTS

Love
ILLUMINATED

INTRODUCTION

LET'S START WITH A QUIZ. BOOKS about love often open with a tantalizing quiz so readers can discover, without too much flipping around, how smart they are, or maybe how stupid the book is.

My quiz won't be the kind where you check your answers against a key to determine your Love IQ. Nor will you be able to upload your responses to an online Personality Pikker® that matches you with a certified LifeMate™ whose compatibility is guaranteed or your money back.

This isn't a book of ironclad answers or money-back guarantees. I will not be locating Mr. Right by GPS, explaining the psychology of why men love bitches, or providing a list of field-tested strategies for entrapping romantic prey. Very little scientific research underpins anything herein because I am not an esteemed doctor or a lauded academic but a lowly newspaper editor, one who—rather improbably, I admit—reads other people's love stories for a living.

At the *New York Times*, I edit a personal-essay column called Modern Love, in which strangers spill their guts about their relationship woes. It's a job I have worked at more or less full-time for the past nine years, a period during which some fifty thousand laments about love have filtered through my brain and, often, my heart.

The stories arrive by e-mail around the clock, pouring into my laptop, dribbling out of my printer, and spilling across the tables of my office and home. They follow me into bed at night, tag along on family vacations, and ping into my iPhone when I'm walking my dogs or standing on the sidelines of my son's soccer games. They also frequently are told to me in person, at cocktail parties, and public events and in planes, trains, and automobiles.

When people find out what I do, they invariably say, "You must know a lot about love." Or they might invoke the name of the newspaper sex columnist played by Sarah Jessica Parker on *Sex and the City* and remark, "You're like a male Carrie Bradshaw."

The first person to make that observation was a journalist who interviewed me early on in my job, when I was so out of the loop love-wise that I didn't even know who Carrie Bradshaw was. I thought the journalist had said, "Terry Bradshaw," the famous Steelers quarterback (now Fox Sports analyst) I'd grown up idolizing during my suburban Pittsburgh childhood. It didn't occur to me to ask what Terry Bradshaw had to do with editing confessional essays about relationships. All I could think was: *I'm like a male Terry Bradshaw? But he is male.*

Shows how little I knew about love back then. Now, nine years later, I apparently know enough about love to fill a book.

Yet I hardly see myself as some guru who sits atop a mountain of accumulated wisdom in my robe and sandals, eager to dispense sage advice to the lovelorn. In my mind I have not been mastering love all these years so much as marinating in it. Asking me what I have learned about love is like asking a pickle what it has learned about vinegar.

Let me try to explain it another way.

Say you're on an ocean cruise, and you're enjoying your narrow experiences and sheltered life, sleeping in your climate-controlled cabin and dining on your private balcony as you gaze out across the ocean, finding it all vaguely pretty as you eat your toast and jam and prepare for your fencing lesson on the lido deck.

That's sort of what my life felt like before I became the Modern Love editor.

Then one night you stumble over the railing and fall into the ocean. But it's not just any ocean—you've fallen into the Sea of Love.

The Sea of Love may sound sexy and appealing when Robert Plant and the Honeydrippers are singing about it, but in reality it's a dark and scary place—deep, cold, impenetrable, and populated by billions of freakish creatures lurking in the depths with their gnashing teeth and electrified appendages. Luckily you'll be stuck in this sea only a short time until your rescue—or so you think. But no one seems to notice your absence, not even your wife, and one day leads to another, and before you know it you've spent nearly a decade in the forbidding murk.

Does all this time in the Sea of Love turn you into a marine biologist who's able to explain why the Caribbean ostracod, a seafloor-dwelling crustacean, uses bioluminescence to attract a mate? Or how the clown fish, a creature of limited mobility, can change its sex from male to female to copulate with a fellow clown fish he brushes up against in his coral cavern?

No, it doesn't. But when you've spent more than a hundred months soaking up the intimate lives of fifty thousand strangers, you can't help but emerge with an education of some kind. Rushing through your head has been a near-constant stream of all the bizarre and mundane things people do in the name of love, from a serial cheater's desperate rationalizations to the baffled regrets of those who seem destined—through insecurity or arrogance or both—to destroy every relationship they ever have.

Of course, amid all the head-scratching tales of frustration and betrayal are equally inexplicable stories of bravery and generosity—hopeful leaps from such perilous heights that you almost have to look away, and courage so vast it makes you feel ashamed of your own timidity. Relationships challenge everyone, but why does desire drive some to benevolence and others to corrosive megalomania?

Let's explore it together. Have you forgotten about our promised quiz? I almost did. Anyway, here it is. Some of these questions might seem a little odd, but then, so is love. Good luck!

1. Do you think it's better to put a lot of effort into finding love, or leave it to fate?
2. If a word like *destiny* makes you gag, should you still try to believe in it?
3. Say you have some physical shortcoming, psychological issue, or medical problem you're embarrassed about that makes you insecure about starting new relationships. When is the best time to inform a new love interest about your perceived inadequacy? Should you come clean early in the relationship and risk scaring the

person off? Or is it better to wait until he or she already has fallen for you?

4. Imagine you're one of an increasing number of couples who met online and never have been together in real life, yet you still feel this is the most important relationship you currently have—the one to which you devote the most time and emotional energy. Do you think a relationship conducted purely online, via words, images, emoticons, and texting shorthand, can be as fulfilling as or possibly even more fulfilling than one conducted in person?

5. Say you are a divorced mother who goes on an online dating service and meets a divorced father from a different city. After an initial e-mail flirtation, you grow close through a series of long, intimate phone calls. He has an odd kind of British accent (he claims he's originally from London), among other appealing characteristics.

Finally, you arrange to meet; he will come to your city at the end of an international business trip. Alas, he calls you distraught from Nigeria, where he was mugged and beaten and is recuperating in a hospital. He has no passport and no money. Might you wire him a thousand dollars as a loan so he can pay his bills and continue his trip and meet you?

Even though this plea sounds alarmingly similar to a lot of spam e-mails you have received over the years, you somehow trust him. After all, this was a phone call, not an e-mail, and it was from your beloved, not a stranger, even though you have never met him. So you send the money, after which he requests more, so you send more, and so on, until you finally accept that maybe you have indeed fallen victim to a con. You stop responding and ignore his pleas until he gives up, but the experience has left you feeling drained and devastated.

Several months pass before you hear from him again, at which point he admits it was a con and begs your forgiveness. He is not a divorced father from England but a single Nigerian man who has never left his country. The thing is, he truly fell in love with you during all those long phone calls, and he still loves you, or so he claims. He explains that he was warned by his criminal bosses not to develop feelings for any women during the seduction phase of the cons, but with you he did anyway, and now he wants another chance. He promises he will never ask you for money again and says he wants to give up his old ways, escape his old life, and meet you. He cannot leave Nigeria, so you would have to go there.

You are wary but in thrall—you fell in love with him, too, and you are still in love with that soft voice, that gentle temperament. You tell yourself it's tragic that poverty has forced him to do such awful work. All you feel for him is affection, but both your brain and your friends are trying to convince you that you are certifiably insane if you proceed with this. You proceed with it anyway.

In the airport, he meets you outside of baggage claim with a smile and flowers, whereupon you burst into tears. You spend day after day together and are happy. He asks you for nothing and cons you out of nothing. But the question remains, whether you're falling for an international con artist or, in a different case, a new crush at your local gym: When people act like they love you, and maybe even say they love you, how can you know if they really do?

6. Congratulations. You have decided to get married and start a family. But like so many people today, you have a hyphenated last name, like Smith-Sullivan, and the person to whom you are engaged also has a hyphenated last name, like Schwartzfelder-Abramowitz. What will you give your children for a last name?

7. Like millions of other bored married people stuck in a midlife rut, you seek out your high school or college sweetheart on Facebook. Soon you find yourself fantasizing about what your life would be like if you had married that person. Like anyone with a libido, you begin to flirt with him or her. Like most people with a family, job, reputation, and friends, you worry about where this might lead.

But you can't stop. And eventually—no doubt inspired by the heroes of romantic comedies who routinely throw caution to the wind and get rewarded for it— you decide to take the plunge and see each other again in person. You are giddy and terrified as the plan takes shape. You slip out of the house with some excuse to your spouse and offspring. On the way to the restaurant (at the halfway point, two hours away), you sense the whole thing is already out of your hands, which is probably for the best, because your hands are shaking. You consider turning around. And then you think: *Why shouldn't I be allowed to feel this kind of passion again after so many years of not feeling it?*

Good question. Why shouldn't you?

8. As a longtime married person, you find yourself won-
    dering about monogamy and questioning its purpose.
    You even have discussions with your friends about how
    sexual fidelity works in the animal kingdom, in which
    only a precious few species are monogamous, among
    them gray wolves and black vultures (you can't help but
    think the foreboding nature of these examples means
    something).

    In any event, you begin to wonder in an urgent way
    what it would be like to kiss someone who isn't your
    spouse. Or just to flirt, for God's sake. Have a drink
    with someone who turns you on and allows you to feel
    the full bloom of desire one more time before you grow
    old and die. Of course, you'd love to actually have sex
    with this person, though that seems kind of unimag-
    inable. But would the other stuff be okay if the oppor-
    tunity presented itself? Where exactly is the physical
    and emotional line that divides remaining faithful from
    cheating?

9. Say your husband or wife experiences a brain-injuring ac-
    cident, falls prey to early-onset dementia, or succumbs to
    a destructive addiction. Like most, you sealed your bond
    years or perhaps decades earlier with idealistic pledges to
    stand by each other during sickness and health and in
    good times and bad.

    Despite your best intentions and efforts in dealing
    with your spouse's diminished abilities and altered per-
    sonality, you find yourself evaluating the future of your
    relationship according to a disturbing calculus of what
    remains versus what's been lost, and of what you hope

you're capable of versus what you fear you aren't. Yes, you promised to be loyal and loving until death did you part. But how far do such promises extend? How much self-sacrifice can love reasonably require? And what happens when the person you promised to love no longer seems to be the person you're married to?

10. Last question. If you're old enough to be interested in this book, you're probably old enough to have experienced love many times in various permutations. Do you think love is primarily a feeling or a choice?

Okay, pencils down. How did you do? Did you find yourself muttering, "I have no idea" to a lot of them? Me too. Bummer, right? How are we supposed to know if we qualify for the Love Mensa Society if we can't even make it through the starter quiz?

Well, keep reading. Those questions will come up again. In fact, they'll serve as leaping-off points (or railings to stumble over) in the ten chapters that follow. I can't promise you all the answers, but answers are overrated anyway. So is advice.

In love, as in life, it's the questions that count. After all, love is about curiosity, not certainty. It's about tossing oneself overboard into the wild seas, not remaining safely on deck. So slip into your wet suit and mask and oxygen tank, and take my hand. Oh, and grab a pair of those rubber nose plugs to keep the salt water from shooting up your nostrils on impact. It's a big drop, and we're going in.

1

Pursuit

SOMEWHERE OUT THERE

HOW DID YOU FIND LOVE? OR, if you haven't found it yet, what's your approach? Are you the type to create lists of desired characteristics, consult experts and dating services, and believe the harder you work at it the more successful you'll be? Or do you think it's better to go about your life as usual, working and socializing and meeting prospective lovers as part of your everyday routine, believing that if it's meant to happen, it will happen? To put it bluntly, are you more of a manic control freak, or some kind of lazy-ass believer in fate?

I confess I fall squarely in the lazy-ass category. And my wife would be the first to admit she tends toward control-freakishness (maybe *proactive* is a better word). Not to blame everything on birth order, but I have to assume my side of the aisle is mostly populated with second-born children like me who are happy to have someone else in charge. And I bet the proactive side has a majority of firstborns like my wife who managed their younger siblings in childhood and then unconsciously seek out the same dynamic in adult relationships.

Cathi and I met more than two decades ago in Tucson, where I was in graduate school at the University of Arizona pursuing a master of fine arts degree in creative writing on a leisurely four-year plan. Though we were the same age, twenty-seven, she had spent her postcollege years ascending editorial mastheads in the New York magazine world and was looking to attend graduate school as a way to slow down so she could write. I, on the other hand, had grabbed my college degree a year later than she did (having been held back in kindergarten) and headed west to Park City, Utah, where I found work as a ski instructor (winter) and janitor (all seasons).

After two years of skiing and mopping, however, I was eager for a fresh challenge, so I decided to head south to Tucson to write short stories under grapefruit trees. Many semesters later, with graduation looming and my future employment looking doubtful, I'd grown so lethargic that by the time Cathi came to town I was having trouble coming up with reasons to leave the house in the morning.

Which is exactly why we met.

True to her meticulous nature, Cathi researches all options before making any decision. So rather than rely on a book or a phone call to get the inside scoop on Arizona's graduate writing program, she got her magazine to fly her across the country on assignment so she could check it out firsthand. After meeting with the program director and probing him for all he had to offer, she asked for the names and numbers of female students who might be willing to share their perspective with her over lunch. She asked specifically for female students because she wanted to hear about a woman's experience in the graduate program, and she also didn't want to have to deal with any weird male-female vibe that might result if she were to take a guy out to lunch.

Since I'm not a woman (and wasn't then either), I don't know why the program director added my name to the end of the list of women he gave her. Whatever the reason, Cathi and I apparently were destined to meet, because none of the women the director mentioned would have lunch with her. They were all much too busy. Whereas when my phone rang on that fateful morning, I was sitting on my bed in a pre-coffee daze, staring listlessly into the void. Free lunch? You bet.

Less than an hour later, over sandwiches and drinks, Cathi began peppering me with questions that were as much about me as the graduate program: "Where are you from? What do you write? Do you have siblings? Roommates?"

Still groggy, I struggled to respond to each one before she'd fire the next: "What's your favorite novel? What magazines do you read? Where'd you get those sunglasses? What are those things that let them hang around your neck?"

Her final request was to see some writing from the program, so after lunch we strolled back to the English department building, where I grabbed a story of mine along with two others from my workshop and handed them over.

The next week, I received a letter from her in New York (yes, an actual posted letter—this was 1989), thanking me for meeting with her and helping her out. She said she'd read my story in her bathtub and loved it. Later—much later—she would tell me her bathtub reading experience was when she first began falling for me. And I would confess that imagining her in a bathtub enjoying my writing was when I first began falling for her.

I wrote back to thank her for the compliments and the lunch, and we began corresponding. Given our contrasting energy levels, my letters tended to be short (two to four pages) while hers stretched as long as twenty pages, single-spaced, often written in the wee hours of the morning before she got up for work the next day. She told me what she'd done at her job, eaten for dinner, read the previous night. She told me about her friends, her exes, the writers she loved, the places she'd traveled. And she asked me about my friends, my exes, the writers I loved, and the places I'd traveled.

In exchanging letters we were trying to figure out, from twenty-five hundred miles away, if we might be right for each other, and soon we were seizing on this detail or that as signs of our romantic potential. For example, we quickly discovered we were born in the same month of the same year (only ten days apart) in the same area of the same small state, meaning we might have taken little breaths of the same air early in our infancy, or spit up onto the same patch of grass or something, which we felt surely boded well for our future compatibility.

And soon we stumbled upon this: My father, who is a political scientist with many books to his credit, happened to dedicate the second edition of one of those books to my brother and me. Cathi's younger sister, then a budding political activist who was taking government courses as an undergraduate at Cornell, had to buy that book for a class. When the semester ended, she brought it home and shelved it in the childhood bedroom she and Cathi shared. Which means that, yes, my name, written by my own father along with the word *love*, was planted in my future wife's bedroom years before we ever met.

Clear proof that she and I are certified soul mates for life, right?

We thought we were, though not just from superficial signs like my father's book or our same-state, same-month birthdays, but because of everything we were learning and doing together by then. Cathi decided to apply to school in Tucson and was accepted, and a few months later, I flew back east to help her move out. We drove across the country in a Jeep we bought together and began living in the same town, eating and hiking and biking together, and taking road trips on holidays and weekends. And while neither of us can say *soul mate* with a straight face (another sign of our compatibility), we did eventually decide that our relationship qualified as love, perhaps even the lifelong variety. For us that meant a combination of mutual attraction, shared sense of humor, similar goals in life (despite my slacker ways, I had glimmers of ambition), and good timing (we were approaching thirty and getting ready to settle down).

Within eighteen months of meeting we were engaged, and less than a year after that we married. Cathi had to be the one to ask me, but I swear I was totally on the verge of asking her.

ROLLING UP OUR SLEEVES TO FIND LOVE

THAT'S HOW CATHI and I found each other twenty-five years ago. Love struck on a day when I could barely muster the energy to leave my house and when she was trying her best to avoid men altogether. And yet through a fluke of circumstance that put my name where it shouldn't have been, combined with an odd convergence of women who claimed to have no time for lunch, our paths crossed.

How do people find love today? Most stumble into it in the same kinds of ways—by crossing paths with someone at school, at work, through friends or relatives, or while sitting in a plane seat or on a park bench. The majority of people I hear from are still finding love in person, whether by accident or referral, without having to brainstorm about more aggressive strategies.

For many, though, that old-school approach hasn't worked. Or they don't have the patience for it. Or they fear it isn't going to be enough. And these days, given all the tools and services available to speed up the frequency (and perhaps even improve the quality) of our romantic path crossing, they don't have to settle for it being enough. Why rely on chance meetings and luck when they can vastly increase their odds of success through sheer effort and determination? That's the attitude I sense from an increasing number of people in the hunt. In fact, one of the more common remarks I hear from the lonely and the frustrated is some version of this resigned sentiment: "I realized I had to start treating my search for love like a job."

Of course, even those who ultimately embrace this idea may be leery of it in the beginning. First, they probably already have a job and neither want nor have time for another. Second, love is supposed to be magical, and most jobs aren't magical, even if you're a magician. And third, while working hard at your job can make you look like a dedicated professional, working hard at finding love can make you look like a desperate loser (or so people worry).

Nevertheless, they press on—some reluctantly, others eagerly—starting with an action plan for their intensified love-finding campaign. Inevitably this plan will mirror the agenda for an office staff meeting, since that's the template most of us are familiar with that comes to strategizing and getting things done (or at least talking about getting things done). And an early item on that agenda usually will be "setting goals and deadlines."

Maybe these proactive daters will pledge to go on at least fifty dates in five months. Or they'll agree to say yes to every romantic offer for a year, which will lead to all kinds of zany experiences. Or they'll promise to join ten online dating sites and contact a hundred people on each, which might involve having brief flirtations with at least a thousand people. (And, actually, didn't Malcolm Gladwell write something about how you have to flirt with at least ten thousand people before you can be considered an expert at love? No, he didn't. But if he had, and it was true, then this plan would get you one-tenth of the way there.)

During the brainstorming phase of a typical office meeting, you can always count on some supervisory drone to urge everyone to "think outside the box" when coming up with their creative solutions (even as his regurgitation of that tired phrase serves as an example of how *not* to think outside the box). And this same rote impulse toward creativity will surface in those who are coaching themselves to be more proactive in their search for love. They'll think: *What I'm doing isn't working. There's got to be a new way, a better way.* And they'll add a few counterintuitive approaches to their love-finding tool kit.

For instance, the obvious strategy these days to accelerate one's love hunt will be to get out and meet more people. But maybe meeting more people isn't the answer. Maybe that's exactly the kind of lazy, obvious thinking they should avoid. An "outside the box" idea, meanwhile, might be for them to isolate themselves with only a few people, like signing up for a monthlong kayaking trip along the coast of Tierra del Fuego with ten complete strangers. Or joining the Peace Corps and being sent off to some far-flung rice paddy with just one or two other like-minded humanitarians. Or figuring out some less exotic method of walling themselves off with only a few contenders for enough time to let love percolate. Because if you only have a handful of people to pick from in the whole world, and you know you have to fall for one of them or nobody, and it's the same deal for them, too, don't you think you'd latch on to someone and make it work? (I didn't just pull the Peace Corps example out of thin air, incidentally. I've actually heard it has a fabulous—if unintended—reputation as a matchmaking organization, boasting impressive marriage rates among its network of globe-trotting do-gooders.)

Office meetings typically wrap up with a delegation of responsibilities, followed by everyone drifting back to their cubicles to lazily troll for answers on the Internet, since that's what's easiest and most efficient. And it's the same with people who decide to roll up their sleeves to find love. After the initial wave of enthusiasm recedes and they realize their more ambitious plans are too exhausting to contemplate, they'll want to turn to some easier approach that doesn't involve having to leave their desk. Which is when they begin clicking around the world of online dating, the one place where proactive daters can feel ambitious and productive while expending minimal energy, at least at first.

Once ridiculed as a sordid meat market for the undesirable, online dating is now the service of choice for searching singles— offering up a seemingly limitless supply of eligible partners like candy on a tree, generating billions of dollars in revenue annually for the industry as a whole and claiming responsibility for hundreds of marriages every single day. Not many years ago your friends might have mocked or pitied you for signing up, but today any mocking is more likely to be directed at those holdouts who refuse to try it no matter what, clinging to their old ways like wilderness survivalists intent on starting a fire by rubbing dry sticks together.

And these sites are not just for young people anymore, if they ever were. The fastest-growing segment of the online dating millions is people in midlife, the divorced and widowed with jobs and kids and routines that keep them busy and away from places where they might meet someone new. For many of them, late at night is the only time to search. And the only place to search is online.

HOW DID WE GET HERE?

IN PREVIOUS CENTURIES people married for many reasons, be they familial, religious, economic, or political. Romantic compatibility, if it was considered at all, was always pretty far down the list. Feelings of love were what you were supposed to develop *after* you got married, or maybe never.

The social upheavals of the past couple of hundred years or so changed all that, and no longer were we going to let outmoded customs or concerns dictate whom we would marry and live with for the rest of our lives. We were going to marry for love! We just needed to devise some reliable and efficient ways of finding it.

Eventually some of our brightest minds at our most esteemed institutions began devoting time and resources to the effort. Research was conducted, results were analyzed, the Internet was invented, everyone got laptops, and before you knew it millions of us were sitting on our butts in the comfort of our own homes searching for the most important relationship in our lives from online catalogs of eager candidates.

This widespread commercialization of matchmaking has not made finding love any less fraught. The basics will always be hard. We don't know if someone we're attracted to is right for us, or if he or she might like us back, and figuring that out might require charm we don't feel we have, time we can't afford, and vulnerability we'd just as soon not have to reveal. Online dating sites don't alleviate those insecurities and pressures, and they never said they would.

The promise of online dating was more like the promise of singles night at the local dance club or bar, but better. Like at a singles night, we would be introduced to a bunch of people we wouldn't meet otherwise, and everybody who showed up was essentially forced to concede their availability up front. With online dating, though, they'd also reveal many other tantalizing tidbits about themselves—their preferences and quirks and relationship history—without everyone first having to small-talk each other to death. So it accelerated the process, and all it would cost us—other than the fee, if applicable—was the time spent sitting at our computers. And let's face it: Sitting at our computers is pretty much all we do anymore anyway. Might as well browse for a spouse while we're at it.

Plus, there were other advantages. Instead of being stuck with the same small pool of unattached losers in your local area, you could choose from among thousands of strangers who were probably more sexy and desirable than the local crowd, since the unknown is always more sexy and desirable than the known (at least until you see pictures or meet in person).

But here's the rub: Since the sites boast far more profiles than anyone can reasonably consider, they rely on various strategies to whittle the candidates down to a manageable group. Ostensibly this group is composed of people with whom you are likely to be compatible.

The entire process operates on the assumption that we know what kind of person we're looking for, and the questionnaire reinforces this, asking who we imagine that ideal person might be and then restricting our dating pool accordingly. As we do this, what began as a rush of enticing possibilities—thousands of them, all within our geographical area!—quickly devolves into a game of exclusion as we flee from variety and risk and mystery and meekly migrate toward the familiar, blackballing entire age groups, races, geographical areas, income brackets, and religions from our dating pool with the click of a mouse.

We can even head straight to a specialized site that "pre-weeds" according to variables such as vocation (FarmersOnly .com), level of attractiveness (BeautifulPeople.com), religion (JDate.com), or age (SeniorPeopleMeet.com), thereby lowering our risk of accidentally ending up in bed with a lawyer, an ugly person, an Episcopalian, or anyone too young to want to meet for dinner at four thirty P.M. in the Leisure Pines cafeteria. And there's nothing to stop our flight, because these aren't real people we're rejecting, but categories.

While real people of various persuasions might have a chance at winning our heart, a category never will. When we make categories our focus, finding love becomes not about limitless possibility but calculated probability. It's less for the dreamer than the schemer.

Chances are we won't hit it off with someone who smokes, so bye-bye smokers. And it seems like the odds of being able to make it work with someone of a different religious background aren't very good, so let's just stick with the faiths we know. When it comes to political leanings, why risk being trapped in a permanent partisan battleground for the rest of your life? Better stay on our side of the aisle for that one, too. And there's no sense in considering anyone who lives more than fifty miles away, not with today's gas prices, so no hopefuls from beyond the stated radius, please.

How about someone who's ten years older? Nah.

Dog in the house? Eh, okay.

Children? No way.

And so it goes, as we eliminate group after group. It makes one wonder: What about those faceless thousands who didn't sync with our preferences? What if our soul mate is among those, and we've somehow barred him or her with our impulsive and somewhat arbitrary choices?

THE TRUTH ABOUT LYING

I WANTED TO see if Cathi and I might have found each other this way, so we signed up with two popular sites—just for research, of course. Well, in my case it was for research; with Cathi, I started to wonder. To explain our single and searching status, I said I was divorced, while she claimed she was widowed yet eager to explore new opportunities for love. Otherwise we answered all of the questions truthfully, though we posted no pictures, which seemed to make us especially intriguing for a while, because we got e-mails begging us for snapshots and were admonished that without pictures we could not take full advantage of our many promising matches.

Unfortunately, those many promising matches that regularly flooded our inboxes did not include each other. No matter how many times I hit "reload," how far I scrolled, or how eagerly I checked my e-mail, Cathi was never recommended as a match for me, nor was I for her. Evidently she had put her sought-after income at a much higher level than the modest amount I'd honestly confessed to. So instead, like a moth to a flame, she was immediately drawn to a "more appropriate" match for her—Leo, a divorced money-market manager with a reported income that was three times what I earn (and probably double what Leo actually earned, or so I suspected).

Is that why Cathi and I weren't recommended for each other—because of our incompatibility over income? Or was it because she'd claimed to be a widow, which meant the computer thought I was dead? After all, a dead person has no salary at all, which, according to their algorithm, would make me an even less suitable match for her than I was as a living person.

Maybe I should have inflated my salary when asked, or at least used my best year instead of my average. Everyone knows that lying is rampant in online dating profiles, especially when it comes to obvious items like age, weight, height, and income. Although some may complain that such widespread lying is a bad thing, not to mention hopelessly shallow (and not a way you want to start a relationship that has to be built on trust), I can't say it seems to matter much in the long run.

Many savvy online daters view this kind of low-grade lying as being like doping in professional sports: i.e., the practice is so pervasive that you can't possibly expect to compete if you don't do it. True, when you dope in sports, you may actually perform at a higher level, but if you arbitrarily chop twenty pounds off your weight and eight years off your age in your dating profile, you're still going to be as heavy and old as you were before you lied. So what's the point?

The point is that the nature and degree of lying on dating websites is so reliably fudged that many online daters just handicap their dates to include the fudging anyway. So the danger is if you tell the truth, people may recalibrate your truthful responses to your disfavor, assuming you're actually older, heavier, shorter, and poorer than you truly are. So in that sense there's a rationale, however twisted, for lying to remain competitive.

OkCupid, a popular free dating site, even tells you exactly how much you might want to recalibrate. For example, men naturally get more sex and attention if they're taller and make more money, so they tend to add two inches to their height (unless they're well over six feet tall already) and boost their incomes by a whopping 20 percent. But it's best not to go overboard, because more seasoned online daters won't hesitate to vent their disapproval if you've grossly misrepresented yourself. Even the most jaded hopefuls still believe in online chemistry, no matter how many times they've been burned in the past. They still approach their date on the park bench or in the restaurant thinking: *This could be it.* So what's the thought that runs through their minds when the person's appearance isn't even remotely as advertised?

They think: *I've been had.*

In the real world, people might feel ashamed of judging someone by looks or age alone, and they might find a way to deal with their disappointment internally, or at least politely. That's not always so in the world of online dating. Before even uttering "Hello," a veteran dater might blurt out something like, "No way you're thirty-two" or, "Just how long ago was your profile picture taken anyway?" Or even if they don't blurt this out, they're thinking it in such an obvious way they don't need to say a word.

If this happens, there's really no point in acting hurt or offended. Nor does it seem wise to overcorrect and get too honest in your profile, confessing how vulnerable and frightened you feel and how this whole process makes you so uncomfortable. Several years ago a Modern Love columnist wrote the following in describing her experiences with dating in midlife: "If we were really honest, our ads would read: My heart has been shattered, and I'm scared. Will someone take a chance on me?"

Tellingly, though, she decided not to mention her tanking IRA and two previous divorces in her own profile. There's a fine line, it seems, between an admission of vulnerability and self-sabotage.

The idea, after all, is to intrigue, not frighten. And unlike meeting in person, when you're processing a whole range of looks, reactions, sounds, smells, and movements and trying to make sense of them, in an online profile you've got two things to go on: words and images. That's what counts. Fair or not, sloppy writing or bad snapshots can doom you before you've even gotten started. Many women I've heard from simply can't continue to correspond with—much less agree to meet—a man who can't spell or who writes in an off-putting style. One woman was so bothered by the guy's habit of never capitalizing or punctuating his messages and relying on texting shorthand that she finally ended their brief flirtation by quipping, "You're too lowercase for me."

To which he replied, "what do u mean"

When it comes to images, which are usually more influential than words, OkCupid has determined that for women, a pouty, up-gazing look generates the most responses, whereas men are encouraged to skip the shirtless shot unless you've got ripped abs, and maybe still skip it even then. Better to pose with a dog or other cute pet—doing so shows you're actually capable of commitment.

Another surprising indication that you're capable of commitment, at least for some: being divorced. As one woman explained, she considered divorce to be a minor plus in scanning profiles because it demonstrated to her—pathetically enough—that the guy had shown his willingness to marry a first time. But being divorced can also cause problems, especially if you and the ex end up on the same online dating site.

Here's what happens. Months or years have passed since your divorce, and you're finally at the point where you have enough distance from the trauma to think about dating again. But you're not young anymore, and most of your social life involves couples and families, on soccer sidelines and at school potlucks, making it almost impossible to meet anyone who's available. You don't really want to expose yourself to the potential humiliation and discomfort of online dating at your age, but it seems like it's either that or nothing.

So you swallow hard and sign up. You have to admit it's a thrill to get your first set of matches. You actually begin to feel excited about your love life for the first time in years. Maybe you *can* start over again. Maybe there *is* someone out there who's at your same stage in life, also a divorced parent, who shares your interests and sensibility.

As you scroll through the grinning mugs of your recommended matches, it turns out there is such a person. It's your ex-spouse.

When you first stumble across the familiar photo and screen name, you don't know whether to laugh, cry, or throw up. On one level it makes sense you'd be matched up—you're basically the same people you were, just older and sadder. But on another level it's downright creepy. You feel like a human version of one of those "You might also be interested in . . ." suggestions based on a customer's history of previous purchases that chirps: "Since you bought x, you might also like y!" Yet there was never any follow-up about how x worked out for you and whether you'd buy that particular product again. You once purchased x, so might you be interested in purchasing it again?

On the less creepy side, at least the computer confirms that you weren't crazy to have married x in the first place. Chemistry.com has confirmed you have chemistry. Or *had* chemistry. Before the two of you blew up the lab.

LOVE BY SEARCH TERM

ALTHOUGH PEOPLE WORRY about the limitations and downsides of online dating, it's really just an opening gambit. It gets us to the drink at the bar, or to the beachside café, after which we move forward in the relationship or not in the same ways we always have or haven't. And even the shallowest impulses such a system might bring out in us, like searching for love according to height or profession, can take us to a deep place anyway. That's the direction love tends to go whether it starts online or not: from shallow to deep. So shallowness does not necessarily beget more shallowness. Which means you may not even be penalized for starting at an absurdly shallow level.

Take the story of Tiffany, who lost her job as a flight attendant during a time of industry consolidation and cutbacks. Although she'd loved the travel perks that came with the job, she wasn't sure, a few years later, if she could handle doing it again, given what the job had devolved into. She'd seen too many flight attendants in ripped hose rushing to McDonald's for lunch— not exactly her dream. But she couldn't help but wonder: What if she were to search for a commercial pilot, fall in love, and wind up with his flight benefits? She had to focus her online search anyway. Why not focus it with one of her greatest wishes in mind?

She decided to give it a shot. Her search quickly identified many pilots, though "pilot" wasn't as focused a term as she had anticipated. First she had to sort through those who were involved in TV "pilot" episodes and a computer programmer who was looking for a "copilot" in life. When she expanded her search, she chatted with one actual pilot who said he was giving up his job with a regional carrier for a gig flying border patrol missions. That was the end of that.

When she took her search national, a flyer who called himself NavyShark caught her eye. He was in the military but planned to leave for commercial jets in a year. But despite months of e-mail exchanges and an actual in-person visit, the chemistry wasn't there, so they parted ways. Next she dated a couple of marine pilots, neither of whom was right, so she gave up and canceled her online dating accounts. And then a friend of hers, a former flight attendant who was also looking for love online and knew of Tiffany's pilot search, told her of an air force flier she'd come across. Should she put them in touch?

Tiffany was game. She wrote to him and they started e-mailing, enjoying the exchange. But he still had ten more years on his air force commitment, plus he planned to stay in the service for years after. And one more thing: He was stationed in the United Arab Emirates.

Didn't matter. First via e-mail, and then in person after he returned, they fell in love. Alas, he had no intention of joining a commercial airline, even if he were to leave the service someday. So instead Tiffany did, landing a flight attendant job for the very kind of low-cost carrier she'd said she'd never work for, and soon she was jetting around the country again.

The working conditions were even worse than she'd expected: runs in her hose and meals at McDonald's were the least of it. But she had found love. For her, searching by category had worked, if not exactly in the way she'd imagined. She and her pilot boyfriend married just as she'd hoped. Only instead of Tiffany getting his flight benefits, he got hers.

FOCUSED SEARCHING VERSUS PERIPHERAL VISION

IN THE END, despite its flaws, online dating obviously succeeds for a lot of people (if you define success, as the sites do, as finding a relationship that leads to marriage). And the success is not limited to the customers alone. As a business, online dating sites are accumulating a treasure trove of data they hope to use to make the process even more successful, more popular, and more profitable. After all, every individual experience, whether failed, successful, or mediocre, leaves behind a data trail of behaviors, preferences, lies, and impulses. And this data is being sifted through and analyzed by businesspeople and academics alike, all of them eager to better understand what works and why, and to reap the dollars that might accompany such knowledge.

Regardless of system, several changes to our dating landscape seem more or less permanent to me. Every day, in selecting every date, millions are now favoring calculation over chance, efficiency over leisure, categories over personalities, and static profiles over the nuances of body language, facial expressions, and unscripted flirtation. In my mind, the more pressing question is not how we should change online dating, but how is online dating changing us? And how might such services be limiting our opportunities rather than expanding them? After all, Cathi and I weren't recommended as matches for each other on either service we tried, even though we ought to be compatible according to many measures.

When we intensify our focus—as online dating sites encourage us to do—we tend to lose our peripheral vision. We may gain a feeling of greater control over our love lives and a sense of mission, but at what cost? By narrowing our romantic choices based on categories, snapshots, and a few written details, do we risk shortchanging ourselves by underestimating the complexity of love? How we meet doesn't matter, of course, but *whom* we meet matters a lot, and our method of searching determines that.

An example: Sophia and her husband never would have found each other on an online dating site. A peace activist in Berkeley who had been arrested several times for political protests, Sophia was antiwar, antiestablishment, and anti-"The Man" in every way. She once trespassed onto a naval base to spray-paint protest messages over the navy's sloganeering billboards. She wore a BREAD NOT BOMBS button. So how did she end up falling in love with a man who's a big-city police officer, former SWAT Team member, and colonel in the army reserve? A man who subscribed to magazines about wound ballistics, called people he didn't like "communists," and distrusted anyone with a beard?

Because her cousin, who was the cop's friend from school, thought she might like him. And much to Sophia's bafflement and consternation, she did. She liked the proper way he looked and acted, his sense of humor, and the way he took care of her. Soon she was alarmed to find herself falling for him despite their on-paper incompatibility. They went through three long years of tearful breakups (usually initiated by her endless second-guessing) while she agonized over how this could work when they were so wrong for each other. And he would hold her hands and hear her out. Then he would say it was true they were different in all the ways she said, but he loved her anyway. They loved each other. So she stayed, because she couldn't quite bring herself to leave.

Soon they married, and their once-opposite lives became enmeshed. After 9/11, his reserve unit was called up for deployment, and Sophia morphed from being "Gandhi girl" (as she put it) to army wife.

Over time, they softened each other's harder edges and illuminated their less informed perspectives, with her understanding and sympathizing with the military life (because she was living it), and him seeking out liberal newspaper columnists and *New Yorker* articles to discuss with her and learn from. And now? After many years of marriage, police service, military deployments, civilian jobs, cross-country moves, the birth of a son, and the adoption of a daughter, they still love each other.

Just like Hyla and Larry, who met in the college library. If Hyla had been able to set dating parameters for herself and blackball categories of unsuitable candidates, smoking would have been at the top of her list of deal breakers. If she had been dating online, she never would have allowed any smokers to infiltrate her dating pool.

People weren't allowed to smoke in her college library, though, which is where she met and got to know Larry. So Hyla didn't find out that the handsome law student who had captured her heart was a smoker until after she'd already fallen into his arms. And when Larry pulled out a pack of Marlboros one day, she couldn't hide her shock and dismay. "You smoke?" she croaked.

He assured her he was quitting.

Did that mean in two weeks? A month?

Yeah, probably.

A year later they were still together: Hyla, Larry, and his cigarettes. Friends asked how she could love a smoker, but she thought: *You can't just choose not to love someone over one bad habit, can you?* Anyway, it was an addiction, not a habit. He was an adorable, lovable guy with an addiction—one he'd promised to quit, by the way, out of his love for her. So they got married. And eventually, after many failed attempts, Larry did manage to quit.

She only had to wait seventeen years.

2

Destiny

MEANT TO BE OR NOT MEANT TO BE?

LIZ WAS DATING A GUY NAMED Bob. The thing about Bob, though, was he had made a conscious decision not to own a car and instead to use only his bicycle for transportation. This was in Los Angeles. Living without a car might have been a healthy choice for Bob and for the environment, but it presented an obstacle for dating, especially in car-centric LA, because Bob couldn't exactly pick up a date on his bicycle and take her anywhere. He either had to meet her within biking distance or rely on her to pick him up and take him places.

Liz liked Bob, but as she tried to figure out if they had a romantic future, she wondered if his intentionally car-free lifestyle was a bad sign.

One evening Liz picked up Bob in her battered Volkswagen, and they headed off to a comedy club on Sunset Boulevard. She had wanted to go to a movie, but he'd really pushed for the comedy club. Bob's lobbying for the comedy club while being unable to drive them there struck Liz as being yet another sign that perhaps this relationship wasn't meant to be.

Upon arrival at the club, they joined the line snaking down the sidewalk toward the entrance. As they waited, they heard the roar of an accelerating car engine coming from behind them. They spun around just in time to see a large 1970s-era car jump the curb and head straight for them.

Liz bolted for the wall of the building, scrambling for safety amid a crush of other club-goers as she felt the car zoom by just inches away. In the confusion that followed, she looked around for Bob. Where was he? And who was that man in the middle of Sunset Boulevard wearing a blue shirt and no pants? Hadn't Bob been wearing a blue shirt? Was the man in the street Bob?

He was. Liz rushed over to find him lucid and ambulatory but badly injured. Help arrived, and off went Bob in an ambulance. Later, in the hospital emergency room, Bob told Liz how he'd been hit by the car, carried on the hood, snagged by his pants, dragged into the street, and deposited there, bottomless. Luckily, though, he had been able to push her out of the car's path just before he was hit.

He did? That's not how Liz remembered it. She remembered scrambling out of the car's path on her own, though it was hard to know for sure: everything had happened so fast. Sure, it was possible Bob had pushed her out of the way. Yet Liz worried that if he had, it would be a sign she should keep dating him, because if you're already dating someone and he saves your life by risking his own, shouldn't your bond grow even stronger, all other factors being equal?

But Liz didn't want their bond to grow stronger. In her ever-evolving calculus of whether or not they were meant to be, most signs were lining up on the negative side. This sign, though, would be a huge positive that might threaten to swamp the negatives.

A reasonable reaction to Liz's story would be to say that if that's how she was thinking about the relationship, she and Bob obviously weren't meant for each other. If you're in love, you're not grasping at signs and weighing pros and cons to decide your romantic future, as if love is some algebraic equation to solve. If you're in love, you're not constantly mulling transportation and entertainment preferences as indicators of compatibility, and you're certainly not thinking that a boyfriend saving your life might actually be a bad thing. If you're in love, you know it!

To which I would say: Yes, some know when they're in love, but others don't. They feel a bond with the person, but they're not sure if that bond reaches the exulted level of love. They have a connection and shared interests. They feel attraction and longing but also a lot of doubt and fear, and they worry that what they feel might not be enough to sustain a lifetime commitment—or anywhere near that long.

We talk about "falling" in love, as if all the process involves is finding the right person, stepping off the ledge, and letting gravity do its thing. But for many, love is more about finding a right-*ish* person and then trying to figure out if what the two of you have together is enough or not. There seem to be, in short, two kinds of love—the kind you can't deny and the kind you eventually come around to. In terms of relationship durability, neither kind seems any more promising than the other. The swooning couple who can't keep their hands off each other might crash and burn in year two or five of marriage, while the deliberative couple that belabored their decision for years may stay together, happily, forever. It's just that those in the first group feel confident about their love going in, and those in the second group don't. So they need to weigh pros and cons and talk about it a lot and seek the guidance of others.

"How did you know it was love?" they'll ask their partnered-up friends.

"We just knew," their friends will reply, maddeningly.

For couples wrestling with this dilemma, signs and a belief in destiny can play a surprisingly influential role in how the couple think about their future. Sometimes these signs are actual behaviors or choices, as they were with Liz and Bob. Other times they're magical coincidences that make a relationship seem destined.

Take the case of Patrick and Jeff, who met during a night of organized speed dating at a New York gay and lesbian center. They liked each other right away. Maybe, Patrick thought, they were even meant for each other. But he was troubled by the unromantic reality of their "how we met" story, which involved locking eyes while sitting on metal folding chairs with numbers pinned to their chests. He had always expected to find his one true love through some magical coincidence, like picking up a dropped glove at the Met and handing it to a stranger who would then steal his heart.

Patrick had other reasons to be wary. He was West Coast mellow while Jeff was East Coast driven. Jeff was Jewish, and Patrick had a long, checkered history of falling for Jewish men only to get his heart broken. Finally, Jeff had confessed he was a "runner," the kind of person who flees relationships when they get hard, while Patrick admitted he was a "willer," the kind of person who tries to will a relationship to work out in a way that sometimes overwhelms the object of his affection. Could a runner and a willer succeed?

They were getting along great, but Patrick was hesitant about getting his hopes up. He wanted a sign from above that they were meant for each other, something that would wipe away the ordinariness and intentionality of their speed-dating origins. Then one evening at dinner Jeff mentioned that he and his family used to go to Chicago to visit his mother's best friend, a woman named Monica Morris.

Monica Morris? Patrick's mother had had a best friend named Monica Morris, too. In fact, his mother used to talk about Monica all the time—she was one of the most influential and memorable friends she'd ever had. Patrick remembered photos of his mother and Monica skiing together at Lake Tahoe. Monica was a bridesmaid in his mother's wedding. Could it be the same Monica Morris?

Nah. First, Monica Morris isn't such an unusual name, and there surely were plenty wandering around. Second, Jeff's mother was a Jew who was born in China, moved to Japan, then Israel, and finally New York, while Patrick's mother (who had died seven years before Patrick and Jeff met) was a Scottish Presbyterian who'd come from Glasgow and lived the rest of her life in San Francisco. There was zero overlap.

Then Jeff invited Patrick to meet his mother at her home on Long Island for Rosh Hashanah, and while they were out at lunch that day, Jeff's mother, as if on cue, started telling Monica Morris stories. When Patrick mentioned the coincidence of his mother's best friend also being named Monica Morris, Jeff's mother was surprised but dismissed any notion that it might be the same person. A little later, though, she began talking about how she'd once visited Monica in San Francisco when Monica was based there as a flight attendant.

"Ma," Jeff blurted. "That's the link. Patrick's Monica Morris is from San Francisco. We are calling her!"

When Jeff's mother called, Patrick got on the phone, introduced himself, mentioned his mother's name, and then asked Monica if she knew her.

"Yes," Monica replied. "She was my best friend in high school."

Patrick wept on the phone as Monica told him stories about his mother that he'd never heard before, stories that briefly brought her back to life for him. This, Patrick thought, was his dropped glove in the Met. This was their connection, their sign. Maybe, despite their red flags and their dull "how we met" story, they were destined to find each other after all, and destined to stay together, too!

They weren't. As the willer and runner they each were, Patrick soon started willing the relationship to be, and then Jeff started running, and that was the end of them. But ever the romantic, Patrick still believed that he and Jeff were brought together for a reason, and that reason was to grant him emotional access to his long-deceased mother through Monica Morris's stories of their childhood friendship, a gift for which he will be forever grateful.

SO CLINGING TO SIGNS DOESN'T ALWAYS work, at least not as you might expect and hope, but sometimes it can provide a well-timed nudge. Consider the story of Natalie, who until she was twenty-three had lived her whole life in Medicine Hat, a small city of sixty thousand in the gas fields in Alberta, Canada. Medicine Hat is actually known as "The Gas City" and also boasts the world's tallest teepee, among many other natural and man-made attractions.

Despite the town's appeal and familiarity, Natalie's young life in Medicine Hat had begun to feel like a narrowing tunnel. She lived with her boyfriend in a house they'd bought together across from where she'd attended high school. She loved her boyfriend, who drove a backhoe and danced a great two-step. And yet as much as she tried to appreciate the comforts and steadiness of her future with him in their house in that town, she sensed there was something else out there for her. What's more, she feared her boyfriend was planning to propose to her on Christmas Day, which was nearly upon them, and then she'd really be trapped.

Instead of proposing, though, he gave her golf shoes, which was at once a relief and also a sign that she really needed to get out of there. So not long after, as much as she was afraid of leaving Medicine Hat and her boyfriend and heading off on her own, she gathered her courage and told him she had to go. And despite his protestations and her fears, she did go, first to the relatively big city of Calgary, where she struggled to make her way for several months, and then on a real global adventure, accepting a job teaching English in Bangkok, Thailand.

Once there, though, she was lonely. She missed home, but she also knew deep down she had been right to leave. In Thailand, as the months passed, she was able to make only one friend, a secretary at the school where she taught. Eager to meet a man and find love but unable to figure out how, she signed up with a Thai online dating service for expats living there (or "sexpats," as Natalie thought of them). But still she had no luck. All of the Western men on the site seemed to be looking for casual sex with Thai women rather than committed relationships with Canadian women (go figure), and not a single person even responded to her. Not until many months later, at any rate, when a fellow Canadian who went by the screen name "Burgundy" contacted her via the site, and they began e-chatting.

His real name was Noel. As they messaged each other, she said his name aloud to herself, liking the sound. Their online chat was going so well she began feeling giddily optimistic. She wanted to meet and said so. Noel replied that he would love to meet, too, but couldn't then because he was heading home soon.

Hopes dashed, Natalie asked where in Canada he was from.

"I grew up in a small town in Alberta," he wrote. "You've probably never heard of it. It's called Medicine Hat."

Natalie choked on her coffee, then read his words again. And she knew. She had had to travel halfway around the world and suffer through months of loneliness and doubt, but this was the sign she'd been waiting for. It just had to be.

And it was. Two years later, Natalie and Noel married and then moved to the mountains of British Columbia, where they still live today.

THE DESTINY EFFECT

ACCORDING TO EXPERTS who have conducted research in this area, huge numbers of us apparently believe in the power of destiny. A Marist poll from 2011 found that a whopping 73 percent of Americans buy into the idea that somewhere out there exists a soul mate (at least one) that we're meant to be with. The experts do caution, however, that when looking for love you might want to keep your soul mate fantasies in check, lest you fall victim to what they have dubbed the "Soul Mate Fallacy."

An article in *Psychology Today* titled "Why You Shouldn't Believe in Soul Mates" makes the sensible point that such boundless idealism can be dangerous during your search because you might expect everything to be natural and perfect with your one true soul mate, and if your time together starts to feel unnatural and imperfect, if you have disagreements and difficulties, then you may conclude he or she isn't "the One" and decide to break up rather than face the hard work relationships require.

And yes, that surely is a concern for those on the front end of love. Diving into any new relationship with childlike naïveté and idiotic expectations certainly can spell doom and is not advisable. But once you're well into the relationship—after you've already done time in the marital trenches and are all too familiar with the gritty, grown-up reality of love—it can't hurt to believe in a higher power, and many even believe that such faith can help them stay together when the going gets tough.

Relationship experts call this phenomenon the "Destiny Effect"—that reservoir of goodwill and positive energy people think they can tap into if they believe their relationship was meant to be. At least, I assumed relationship experts would have called it something like that by now—it's just too obvious, don't you think? Alas, when I typed *destiny effect* into Google, the only uses of the name that surfaced were for a card trick, a Christian youth group, and a garage band in rural Colorado. So it looks like I'm out on a limb with this one, and if you choose to believe in the Destiny Effect with me, please realize you'll be doing so without the backing of the broader scientific community.

I do know this: Whether or not the Destiny Effect has been trademarked by the US Patent Office or approved for use by the FDA, many of us want to benefit from its magical balm of reassurance, especially when doubts and disagreements start to tear at the fabric of our relationship. Reason and lust have their place in finding love, but if possible we also want to feel like our relationship was maneuvered into place by forces greater than our own humble brainpower and raging libido.

Waiting around for the hand of fate to steer us into love is easy as long as we have plenty of time. After all, not forcing things is what being a fatalist is about, allowing your life to unspool naturally and meeting prospective lovers as part of your everyday routine until that magical moment when you find yourself standing side by side with your one true love. Like Patrick, what fatalists really want is the equivalent of a dropped glove at the Met, some happy accident or encounter that tells them whom they should be with.

Maybe it's securing that last seat on the flight to Detroit that puts them shoulder to shoulder with their future spouse. Or perhaps it's when they lose their phone on the subway, call the number to see if anyone has found it, someone says, "Hello?" and a few years later, the two of them are pushing a stroller together.

The downside of this approach, though, is you can't speed it up if time is short. You can hardly be buying extra airline tickets and leaving cell phones on train seats to find love, and if you do you're kind of forcing fate anyway, right? So what can you do if you're a fatalist at heart but need to accelerate the magic? Are there ways to find love fast but fatefully? To seek destiny on a deadline?

Yes, there are ways. Do they work? Sometimes!

SO WHAT'S WRONG WITH YOU?

PEOPLE HAVE VARIOUS reasons for being in a hurry to find love: a ticking biological clock, the realization they're going bald or losing their youthful appeal in other ways, the pressure to do what everyone else is doing . . . even just an urge for a house and dog and someone to share them with. The typical anxious singletons who send their stories my way are in their late twenties or early thirties. The vast majority are neither shut-ins nor agoraphobics, neither physically nor socially undesirable, neither sexually awkward nor inexperienced. They don't live in basements or caves where they subsist on cat food and vodka. They aren't more obsessed with marriage than others (and often are less so, which is why they haven't already forced a relationship that didn't feel right). Despite what much of the love-finding literature will urge, they probably don't need to "fix" something about themselves, like become extroverted if they are introverted, laugh at jokes they don't think are funny to "show personality," or follow some artificial list of dating rules that runs counter to what their heart is telling them to do.

A woman I heard from who was single into her thirties, and during one bad stretch hadn't had a date in years, dreaded having to confess to a new man about her romantic drought. One time when she did, the guy actually said—tactlessly, yes, but with an air more of curiosity than judgment—"So what's wrong with you?"

But there was nothing wrong with her. Or more accurately, there was nothing *more* wrong with her than there is with anyone. She didn't know it then, but eventually she would find love, and she would learn that she just hadn't met the right person yet. Focusing on what might be "wrong" with her wasn't the point. And that's the case with almost anyone who's feeling unwanted and hopeless. They simply haven't met the right person. And some people never do. But that still doesn't mean something is more wrong with them than there is with millions of other people who do find love.

Like most of their friends and peers, those who feel the need to speed up their search probably have spent the past ten to fifteen years meandering through a series of relationships, had their heart broken and broken the hearts of others, and also drifted along in several arrangements, platonic or not, that were fun, comfortable, one-sided, or all three, but went nowhere. And then the game of marital musical chairs among their age group suddenly drew to a close, leaving them with no place to sit.

They feel baffled and frustrated to be in this position. They always assumed love would happen naturally, and as the romantics they are, they bridle at the prospect of having to go out and find it unnaturally, through some system that will cost them in time and probably money, require yet another user name (lonely jane2346) and password (pleAseG0D), and ask that they complete a brief personality analysis with questions that can feel odd and invasive: "Which pubic-hair style do you prefer for a partner? Natural? Neatly trimmed? Completely shaven? Don't care?"

Faced with this electronic inquisition, they can't help but think wistfully back to Lover X from their past, the kind of person who might have worked out if the timing had been different—someone who now makes them wonder if they were expecting too much or being too picky back then. Lover X, of course, recently married someone else, having long ago moved on. And it's not really envy they feel at this missed opportunity (they had their chance, after all) but self-loathing, a berating voice in their head telling them that this is what they get for thinking there always would be a better match out there, that they had plenty of time, that love really had to feel like LOVE for them to grab hold and hang on. How could they have been so stupid?

The truth is, a generation or two ago there's a decent chance they would have married Lover X. Back then such a relationship probably would have been deemed good enough, and the timing might have been right, too, because they wouldn't have thought they had another five or ten years to keep looking for someone better. And odds are they wouldn't have had so many people to choose from in the first place because all kinds of prejudices, laws, practicalities, geographical considerations, religious customs, and family meddling narrowed their choices. Interracial marriage was flat-out illegal in some states, as were other frowned-upon pairings. Depending where you lived, if you had your heart set on tying the knot with someone who had tuberculosis, say, or was considered by some official measure to be "feeble-minded," you could just forget about that because it was against the law. To remain a citizen in good standing, you needed to get serious and pick somebody from the approved list, please.

Although laws and prejudices continue to circumscribe our choices—opposition to gay marriage being the obvious example—other walls have come tumbling down, and we seem to be headed in that direction with gay marriage, too. All told, we're fast reaching the point where most of us think we ought to be allowed to marry whomever we please, as long as there are only two of us and both are adults capable of consent.

This increase in freedom, though, can bring with it a burdensome flip side. When we can choose anyone from almost anywhere and it's completely up to us, the pressure to make the "best" choice can feel overwhelming, and the chance that we might later feel disappointed with the choice we make grows—at least during times of stress and conflict—because just look at all the others we passed up. And what's most troubling, of course, is the possibility that we already missed out on the person we realize (in retrospect) we were meant to be with, only we weren't mature or ready or whatever enough to know it, and now it's too late. I've read many painful, bewildered accounts of people who broke up with those they later claimed to have loved simply because they couldn't figure out if what they felt at the time was enough to be sure. And they wonder if "being sure" is even possible.

Part of the issue, too, is there's less incentive to commit or marry than there used to be, especially for women. In many cases they feel so self-sufficient on their own and so leery of marriage that they must work to convince themselves that getting hitched is in their best interest. It can be easier financially to raise a family with two incomes instead of one, but the rest can be handled alone if that's not an issue: Women no longer even need a man to be physically present to make babies and increasingly are doing so on their own with sperm banks, artificial insemination, and surrogates (along with a healthy bank account).

When marriage is no longer about baby making, financial need, or acquiring another set of hands to help work the farm, we can be more demanding in terms of what the other person must bring to the table. And what many require as a baseline is the Deluxe Dreamboat Package: mutual adoration, great sex, compatible tastes and sense of humor, impressive earning power, and evolved views on shared parenthood and housework. On top of that, we'd like a dollop of soul mate, please—someone who gets us on every level. It can feel like an impossibly high standard.

DESTINY ON DEMAND

THOSE WHO BELIEVE in destiny are often suspicious of the commercialization of love. They don't trust high-volume matchmaking systems, whether they involve online dating or in-person speed-dating sessions. Instead they tend to be throwbacks to an earlier time when dating pools were small and all love was local. So when looking to speed up the hunt, they are more likely to turn to throwback methods as well, such as fortune-telling traditions that have existed for centuries.

They didn't want to be control freaks about their love lives when they had plenty of time, and they don't want to become control freaks now that time is short. What they want is for someone else to be in control, someone who will tell them whom to love, where to look, or in what way to open their heart.

Nearly all of the following options are old-fashioned and decidedly unscientific, yet many deliver on their promises, if not exactly in the way you might expect. Let's start with the least realistic and work our way forward.

Arranged Marriage

There is no better way of putting your relationship in someone else's hands than by agreeing to an arranged marriage—that age-old, patriarchal, dowry-exchanging custom still practiced in many cultures around the world, though not, generally, in this one. Given our lack of an arranged-marriage tradition, I've been surprised to hear so many frustrated love seekers yearn for it. Or maybe that's precisely why it's such an enticing fantasy; it's easy to long for something you know will never happen.

So what's the appeal? For starters, low expectations. After all, it's hard to have high expectations—or any—when you don't even know the person. In contrast, Western marriages tend to begin with stratospheric hopes. We believe we have found true love at last, and now we finally can revel in our bliss. So as soon as dissatisfaction or unhappiness creeps in—and it will—we are surprised, upset, and maybe already contemplating whether we made a "mistake" we need to undo, and fast.

Consider Farahad's story. As a young man in India, Farahad approached his future marriage with a shrug. A software developer who traveled internationally, he knew his mother would pick out his bride for him, and he knew she would pick someone who was appropriate in terms of religion as well as social and economic standing. When she asked him for his input one day, he was surprised even to be consulted in the matter, and after thinking a moment, he requested only that his bride be a college graduate who spoke English. Otherwise, he blithely replied, "Whomever you choose."

As it turned out, his mother already had a local girl in mind. Her one concern was that he marry a girl from their village, the logic being that his job would likely lead him to live abroad (India's fledgling software industry was too undeveloped then to hold him), and she didn't want his short visits home each year to be divided between their town and wherever his wife's family lived. She wanted him to be able to come to one town for both and not waste time traveling between.

So it was decided: English-speaking, college graduate, and local. The girl Farahad's mother had already chosen, Sameera, fit the bill, and that very afternoon they rushed off for an impromptu meeting at her house, during which they chatted and ate bread. Upon returning home, Farahad nodded his approval to his mother, having appraised Sameera as being cute and confident. Sameera apparently liked him well enough, too.

That was twenty years and two sons ago. Before marrying, Farahad and Sameera had met for a total of forty-five minutes. After they married, their courtship began in earnest: they went out to the movies and the beach, fought and made up, had sex and fell in love. As Farahad explained, "The slow discovery of another person and the unraveling of layers of mystery are part of the fun of arranged marriage." That process of discovery is ostensibly the fun of courtship, too, except that in arranged marriage the goal is to figure out *how* to be married, not *whether* to marry.

Farahad's positive take on his arranged marriage is no outlier. Nearly every arranged-marriage story I've seen has followed a similar arc and was told with a nearly identical tone of humble appreciation. The couples began their marriages expecting to have to get to know each other, to come to love each other over time, and to somehow make it work. As improbable as it may seem, they very often do. And part of this is surely due to the fact that instead of starting out at a peak of love and then watching in anxious disbelief as the marriage deteriorates over the years into a thankless grind (for some), they begin with a blank slate and, if they are lucky, are able to gaze upon their life in wonder as warmth and affection take hold and flourish in the unlikeliest terrain.

Neither trajectory, of course, is certain or even probable. Plenty of besotted newlyweds soar to even higher highs as their love evolves and grows, just as many arranged couples sink to even lower lows as the magnitude of their mismatch becomes apparent. But those who begin with no feelings at all for each other clearly have a greater potential upside, at least according to the "buy low, sell high" mantra of long-term investing. Not to be so crass as to equate love with the stock market, but what is marriage if not a long-term investment? All love is a leap into the unknown, argue practitioners of arranged marriage. Theirs is, too.

An even bigger leap, though, is offering yourself up to an arranged marriage when you don't come from an arranged-marriage culture. That's what many of the Moonies did in the glory years of the Unification Church when they agreed to wed a total stranger from another country, someone randomly selected (by the now-deceased Reverend Sun Myung Moon) and to whom they were married off in ceremonies of thousands, all to advance the cause of global peace by having children whose creation and existence was meant to symbolize bridged international divisions.

Renee was a Moonie who went this route, but for her it proved to be a leap too far. Married to a complete stranger from Japan in a mass wedding in the grand ballroom of the New Yorker Hotel in the spring of 1987, Renee had decided to commit to their union no matter what. In marrying Renee and her husband, the Reverend Moon had selected them from among hundreds.

After she and her husband were pulled toward one another by their shirtsleeves, the Reverend Moon said, "I put you together not for your own happiness but for the beautiful children your marriages will produce." Which could be interpreted both as a fair warning at the time and as a useful rationalization later, should they need one. The message being: Don't plan to be thrilled with how this goes. And if you aren't, you can tell yourself that this isn't supposed to be about your happiness anyway.

This kind of sublimation worked for Renee, and she and her husband had three children and managed to stay together for eighteen years. Until finally, despite all of her effort and hope, she knew she had to get out. But how could she do such a thing? How could she break her vow? Contemplating the possibility made her feel selfish and guilt-ridden.

Appropriately, though, in a marriage whose purpose had been to create beautiful children who were symbols of peace, it was one of those children, her twelve-year-old daughter, who essentially released Renee from her commitment. Aware of her mother's turmoil and pain, she said, "Maybe God put you and Daddy together to have the three of us. And maybe now it's okay for you not to be married."

With this permission, Renee did eventually divorce, and in time she found real love with a new man, and so began her second life.

Even if you can't imagine yourself marrying some stranger who was selected for you, there are still lessons to be learned from arranged marriage. The most important one I've seen is for us to approach love and marriage more humbly than we often do, with our starry-eyed expectations of lifelong romance and connection and great sex. We believe those things are requirements for love, the foundation of a successful marriage, the spring from which all good things flow. But we can very easily come to marriage with an abundance of connection and affection and then lose it, just as we can come to marriage completely empty-handed and build it.

Religious Gurus

Not all religious gurus in the matchmaking business pick spouses and perform mass weddings. Some are simply fortune-tellers of the nonprofit variety. What if you're not religious? Not a problem. You don't have to be to benefit from the matchmaking wizardry of a religious guru.

I didn't even know such a thing existed until Amy told me her story. A thirty-eight-year-old nonreligious Jew, as well as an accomplished writer and journalist, Amy had reached the point where she had to admit to herself and to others that she wanted to get married and have a family before it was too late, if it wasn't already.

While on a soul-searching trip to Israel to take stock of her life, she had a conversation with one of her friends' mothers, who insisted Amy go see a Kabbalist rabbi who had predicted all of her daughters' marriages (and also had saved her husband's life, but that's another story).

Figuring she had nothing to lose, Amy went to visit the rabbi. The encounter didn't begin auspiciously. The man had a beard so long Amy couldn't see his mouth, and his glasses were so thick they nearly obscured his milky eyes. What could such a man know about love? Nevertheless, she confessed to him that, yes, she wanted a husband. And she had come to him for help in finding one.

The rabbi demanded she pay him four hundred shekels (then the equivalent of about one hundred dollars, which he would give to charity) so that he could give her a marriage blessing and predict the circumstances and timing of when she would meet her future husband.

Amy didn't have four hundred shekels. The rabbi insisted she go to the ATM to get it, and he even told her exactly where the nearest one was. At that point she figured she was being hustled anyway, but she found herself robotically following his instructions, against her better judgment.

When Amy returned with the money, the rabbi took the cash, placed it in a Ziploc bag, and then explained to her that the reason she was still alone was because she had been cursed, and the first thing he had to do was lift that curse. After doing so, he told her she soon would meet a man who would please her sexually, give her children, and love her more than he loved his mother.

Sounded good to her. But how was she supposed to meet this man?

It would be done on Hanukkah, he explained.

She thought: *That's only four months away!*

"Done," he repeated, "on Hanukkah."

She both believed him and didn't. The whole thing seemed like such a scam, yet her friend's mother had vouched for him.

After returning to New York, Amy remained skeptical of the rabbi's promises. But that Hanukkah she was vigilant. Her heart was open. She scrutinized every man she met. *Is that him? Or that one?* But Hanukkah passed and nothing happened. She met no one who seemed right or even close. Yet an odd thing had taken place: She realized she had been actively open to love during the entire holiday. She was crushed now, but at the time, despite her skepticism and pessimism, she actually had opened her heart to the possibility of love with nearly every man she met.

A full year passed. Another year of no soul mate and no love. As the holiday approached again, she was struck by another thought: The rabbi hadn't specified which Hanukkah. He'd just said, "Done on Hanukkah." So maybe he meant this one?

Admittedly grasping at straws, she opened her heart once again to every man she met. She appraised each guy she encountered during the holiday, thinking, *Him? Maybe him?* And of course it was at a Hanukkah party, just as she was about to leave (yet again feeling lonely and hopeless), that a guy she'd glimpsed earlier but hadn't yet spoken to approached out of the darkness and said, "Where are you going? Don't leave yet."

So she didn't leave. And now that man, Solomon, is her husband.

Did the rabbi really predict it? Or did his prediction simply cause her to make it so? Amy will never know. And she doesn't really care.

Psychics (and Other Fortune-tellers)

Say you can't afford a trip to Israel. Or maybe you find the idea
of a religious guru with milky eyes and a scraggly beard giving
you love advice too disturbing. In this case you might be a great
candidate for consulting a psychic (or a tarot card reader, astrol-
ogist, palm reader, etc.). If you bridle at this suggestion because
you don't consider yourself the kind of person who would consult a psychic about your love life, you're in good company. In
my experience, no one who visits a psychic about love thinks
they are the kind of person who would visit a psychic about love.

Second, if you're actually visiting a psychic about love when
doing so is the last thing you'd ever consider, you've probably
already reached that tipping point on your scale of desperation
where you are officially open to trying new things, meeting new
people, and therefore believing in love. Any savvy psychic surely
knows this: that you are an open vessel, awaiting direction. The
fact that you have entered this state is good not only for the psychic but possibly for you as well.

With the psychic's assistance, you may just be successful this
time. Though if you've been following me, you might already
understand that the psychic is, in my view, merely a bit player in
this drama, a catalyst, and you are the agent of your own change.
It may seem like you're yielding control, but in reality you're
taking control by believing you're yielding it. It's a mind game,
but it can be a mind game that actually works.

Why? Sometimes I get the feeling we've busted this love
thing so wide open with our endless array of choices that many
of us simply can't cope. We are so distracted and anxious and
even paralyzed by choice we can't make a move in any direction.
In other areas of our lives, those who are overly distracted and

anxious and feel paralyzed by choice take drugs like Ritalin and Adderall to help them cut out the noise and focus.

For overwhelmed and despairing singletons, a psychic (or anyone with any aura of fortune-telling authority) can serve as a dose of relationship Ritalin, getting the lost lover to focus in a certain direction, or on a window of time, or on a specific kind of person. Their message is: Pay attention now. Go to locations *x*, *y*, and *z* during time frames *q* and *r* and keep your eyes and heart open. And love will happen.

After we published Amy's story about the rabbi's successful prediction, she and I were inundated with pleas asking for his name and contact information. Not just the Monday after the piece ran, or the following week, or over the next month or two. For *years* we continued to receive such queries. And this was for a rabbi who lived half a world away in Jerusalem. People twitching for a dose of relationship Ritalin were considering a trip to Israel or were already on their way, *thrilled* to fork over four hundred shekels for something—anything—to grasp on to when it comes to finding love. This wasn't an anomaly. Every time we publish a story about psychics or fortune-tellers who seem to have a track record of success in predicting romance, the queries pour in.

As a natural skeptic of such services, I have now seen enough to make me a believer. Not in the magical powers of psychics and fortune-tellers, but in their ability to get us to pay better attention to the world we're already living in, or sleepwalking through. Hiring a fortune-teller actually can be a pretty cheap way to find love, all things considered. And as a bonus, your visit and follow-through can make for a colorful "how we met" story.

RETROACTIVE DESTINY

ONCE UPON A time, a woman I knew opened a fortune cookie and pulled one that read, "A bald man with a beard will change your life." Lo and behold, she did meet a bald man with a beard, and he changed her life. In fact, he asked her to marry him. And they went on to have two sons and live a happy and prosperous life together. Not too long ago they celebrated their fiftieth anniversary.

Except he wasn't actually bald when they met. And he didn't have a beard either. He was a young man with a full head of hair and scrubbed cheeks. In reality, she didn't stumble upon that fortune until two decades later, and by then, of course, he had become bald and bearded, which is why she found the fortune so charming, despite its chronological inaccuracy.

To be chronologically accurate, the fortune would have to read: "A bald man with a beard *has* changed your life." Although in that case it would not be fortune but fact.

No matter. The message touched her anyway, so she saved it. She saw it as yet another piece of evidence, however erroneous, that she and her husband were meant to find each other all those years earlier. This is what I mean by "retroactive destiny." If we don't start with magic, we can find ways of manufacturing it later.

In this case, though, I personally can vouch for destiny's role in their pairing. The woman who saved the fortune is my mother. The bald man with the beard is my father. And if they hadn't met, I wouldn't exist. And if I didn't exist, you'd be reading a book of blank pages right now. And why would you be doing that?

It makes no sense. Nobody reads a book of blank pages.

So you see? The only story that makes sense is the one in which my mother and father met and fell in love and created my brother and then me.

As if, you know, it was their destiny.

3

Vulnerability

OH, AND BY THE WAY . . .

YOU FINALLY FOUND SOMEONE YOU MIGHT love. It's only been a little while, and you don't want to get your hopes up, but this seems promising. You haven't even gotten physical yet. You don't really know each other, and you're walking on eggshells, looking for "signs" and worrying that any misstep might derail things.

Given the precarious phase you're in, when do you think might be the best time to break the news that you have herpes, or alcoholism, or the fact that you were born with only one testicle, as was the case with one man who wrote to me? Mr. One Testicle seemed particularly perplexed over the timing of his disclosure, because wouldn't blurting it out apropos of nothing when they hardly knew each other be incredibly awkward, bordering on creepy? Yet he also didn't want to wait until he and his new love interest were naked under the sheets together and the situation was suddenly (ahem) at hand.

One woman had come up with a hard-and-fast rule about when to confess her bisexuality: on the third date. And she stuck to it, without fail, though she dreaded having to say the word every single time. She felt that a potential lover ought to know about such an important element of her identity sooner rather than later. But was she making too big a deal of it? Did it really matter so much? And how was the person supposed to react? This kind of disclosure dilemma, for most people, seems to involve finding the sweet spot, that perfect moment in the progression of their relationship when they believe their love interest is invested enough to keep caring but not so invested that he or she is going to feel lied to (or even betrayed) by the delay.

I realize most of us aren't agonizing over bisexuality confessions or one-testicle disclosure issues. But we all have failings and insecurities—physical and emotional scars, divorces, STDs, cancer—that we're trying to hide or at least de-emphasize early in a relationship. I've heard from chemotherapy patients who have agonized over the "wig reveal" and from someone with a disfiguring leg disease who agonized over her "pants reveal."

I can't say when the best time is to come clean and become fully vulnerable in a relationship; no one can. What I can say is what everyone already knows or should: Vulnerability is what love is all about. And vulnerability involves yielding control, revealing weakness, embracing imperfection, and opening ourselves up to the possibility of loss. Only when we open ourselves to the possibility of loss can we allow for the possibility of love.

Our approach to finding love in the twenty-first century, however, is often more about tightening our control, avoiding mistakes, airbrushing our flaws, and putting ourselves ever more firmly in the driver's seat of our romantic lives. What's unnerving about love today is the extent to which we're exploiting technology to try to avoid vulnerability altogether, as if we have somehow evolved to the point where we now can have love without it.

We might choose to criticize those who won't or can't commit to us by saying they have a fear of commitment, deflecting the pain of their indecision or rejection by suggesting they're incapable of committing to anyone, not just us. In the past this term was mostly reserved for bachelors who refused to settle down no matter what, heartless cads who were unable to forge a lasting relationship even with a dog, cat, or gerbil for fear that any creature with a beating heart might prevent them from being able to rollerblade all day and party all night, tying them down physically and emotionally in ways they couldn't stomach.

(Now, of course, along with all the other ways women are matching or surpassing men, they are also catching up in the heartless cad category. Among my fifty thousand strangers, I see almost as many women who supposedly can't commit, and in those nonrelationships it's the men who are trailing along, clinging to whatever scraps of hope they can despite the constant stiff-arm they receive, before ultimately being cast off.)

When you have been held at arm's length or dumped by a so-called commitment-phobe, it may be cathartic to dismiss him or her as being immature, selfish, withdrawn, cold, narcissistic, and probably beyond rehabilitation. Yet many are simply afraid. They gaze across the minefield of marriage and parenthood and don't see any safe route to the other side. They know that eventually somebody is going to step on a mine, and when they do, there will be significant losses. So for now they're content to wait at the edge, even as friends, peers, and siblings all venture forth into that open field laced with hidden dangers.

Remain at the edge or walk forward into the field—those are your choices. In seeking love, you can either insulate yourself from love and loss by remaining aloof, or you can expose yourself to love and loss by being vulnerable. And then there is a third way, a middle way, which is to walk into the open field wearing armor, to take baby steps toward risk and vulnerability while also trying to protect your weakest flank.

ACTING ALOOF: FROM THE TERSE TEXT TO THE HOLLOW HOOKUP

COMMUNICATIONS TECHNOLOGY AND ever-loosening attitudes about sex and commitment are providing countless new opportunities to act aloof in relationships. In fact, acting aloof is so common these days that sincerity and vulnerability, for many, can start to feel disgusting and unnatural, like wearing a suit when everyone else is dressed in ripped shorts and sandals.

I can't tell you how many times I've heard of young women being creeped out by men who expressed affection a little too openly or earnestly for their taste. It often seems like what used to be called chivalry—a man helping a woman to remove her coat in a restaurant, for example—can now be seen as coming on *way* too strong. And the term *stalker* has been watered down to the point where confessing that you really like someone might qualify.

A cautionary note: I cannot personally recommend acting aloof in relationships, not for very long anyway. I acted aloof for almost a decade, throughout high school, college, and for several years after, not out of some strategy of seduction but simply from a fear of rejection. And I regret all those lost years and stunted relationships. To each his own, though, and if you choose to act like you don't care about anything or anyone, at least for a while, here are some of the techniques you might try to hone your skills.

Booty Texting (and Booty Grazing)

Some people seem to view casual sexual relationships as just another product to procure online with their smartphones while they're sitting around feeling anxious and lonely. They tend to go about their shopping compulsively but dispassionately, moving from one possibility to the next until their order is fulfilled and they can proceed to the checkout with their virtual shopping cart of prearranged sexual encounters. This is the world of the "booty text."

The online Urban Dictionary defines a *booty text* as: "A late-night summon via text message, instead of calling, in order to engage in sexual activities. Most commonly used when you are very horny and in a situation where you cannot use your cell phone to make a call."

Drafting long text messages can take time, and reading long texts—depending on your device and eyesight—can be wearying, so there are practical reasons to keep your message short. But convenience is not the only benefit of brevity, especially for those who are trying to act aloof, because the shortness of your message also can be used to show just how little you care.

However you pitch your encounter, you'll want to convey that it doesn't matter much to you whether the sex happens or not. Rejection won't bother you. In fact, whatever disappointment you experience will last only as long as it takes you to send out your next text. And because these exchanges mostly take place among young men and women who (supposedly) aren't looking for more than a casual sexual encounter, it's not demeaning to either party. The person who receives the text is also trying to act aloof in relationships, or so it's assumed.

Another way to reinforce your lack of caring is to make the text as generic as possible, omitting names and any relationship-specific details so that you can retext it elsewhere without revision. This "dear occupant" approach to booty texting is called *booty grazing*, a term that appropriately evokes the image of a cow dumbly chomping on grass all day, the message being that when you're booty grazing you choose among potential sex partners with almost the same lack of discernment as a cow choosing among blades of grass.

The irony is that, as with any worthy writing project, it may actually require more time and creative energy to write it short than to write it long. So it's a good thing the recipient of your booty text has no way of knowing how long you spent, or he or she might mistake that extra investment of time and intellect for caring. Here's my example, which took me almost an hour: "ur gr8 lets m8." (If you can't figure out the phonetics, my appeal reads: "You're great. Let's mate.")

If you get a positive response—"lol its f8!"—then you've done it: you have summoned sex to your doorstep (or gotten yourself summoned to someone else's doorstep for sex) while demonstrating the least effort and care possible. Such is the beauty and efficiency of booty texting. Isn't it great being clever and shallow and not ruining something as potentially awesome as meaningless sex with all that stupid emotional turmoil?

It definitely can be. Just be aware, however, that no matter what your cell phone contract stipulates, booty texting plans are rarely unlimited. The overage charges may not show up on your monthly bill, but if you're a heavy user, it may still cost you dearly in ways both predictable and not.

Sending Dick Pix

People often joke that horny men think with their penises, or that a man's brain actually is located in his genitalia at certain times. While some men might take offense at this, others give the joke credence by using texted or e-mailed snapshots of their all-beef thermometer to represent them in their attempts to find love, meaning these men are essentially letting their baloney pony determine their romantic choices for them, much as a brain would.

Sending pictures of your man-muscle to strangers via the Internet involves exposing yourself, obviously, but not in a way that makes you feel vulnerable. On the contrary, texting your Twinkie is usually about feeling *in*vulnerable. Sound counterintuitive? Let's look at a real-life example.

Say your name is Anthony Weiner, you're a nationally known politician with grand ambitions, and you decide to send pictures of your wiener to a woman who's not your wife, even when it's blindingly obvious how such an act might play out in the press, given your notoriety and comically relevant name. And then, after you're exposed and humiliated and forced to resign for doing this the first time, you fall right back into sexting with strangers, setting the stage for a second round of exposure and humiliation. Considering the risks, do you think your decision to bare all would be driven more by humility or bravado?

(With thanks to the Online Slang Dictionary for helping me avoid saying "penis" seven times in four sentences.)

Hooking Up

Though it may be easy and popular to blame our increasing aloofness in relationships on technology, that's only part of the story. The hookup culture so common on college campuses, in which students prefer casual sexual relationships (as one-night stands or as ongoing "sex only" arrangements) over more committed and emotionally grounded couplings, is a case study in vulnerability avoidance.

In the two Modern Love college essay contests I've held, nationwide events that drew thousands of accounts of what college students are dealing with and questioning about love and relationships, hooking up was very much on the students' minds. Though some wrote with remarkable maturity and style, the majority of essays were not particularly accomplished or, in some cases, even very readable. But often the students' lack of artfulness and awareness tended to be even more revealing as they laid bare their stories and emotions, from the trauma of date rape to the alienation of pornography to the awkward dance of acting like they didn't care about someone they had come to care about.

What they revealed, intentionally or not, was how hooking up involved an attempt to neatly separate the physical from the emotional, to experience sexual pleasure while ignoring or suppressing emotional connection. Its rule book seemed to state:

Have fun but don't feel. Don't expect anything and don't care. Simple as that. Except for many, of course, it's not so simple. For many, the emotional part is roiling but clamped down because hooking up is not supposed to be about that.

Some have praised hooking up as a sign of women's increasing power and independence, the argument being that young women now prefer casual sex on a par with men as a means of keeping themselves free from entanglements so they can focus on their studies and careers. An actual relationship would drag them down with emotional baggage and be a drain on their time and energy, and they don't want that, at least not yet, because the potential mess would threaten to knock them off the trajectory they've long imagined for their lives. With hookups, they get the fun without the distraction.

Theoretically, this explanation sounds reasonable enough; I've heard young women claim as much plenty of times. The only problem is we don't live our romantic lives theoretically. We live them in real situations with real people. And we don't always end up feeling the way we want to feel just because we find certain notions of independence and careerism appealing. Sometimes we actually, you know, fall in love when we don't expect or intend to. Attachments can bloom at the most inopportune times—like during a hookup. And deciding to squelch these inconvenient feelings is hardly empowering or liberating for young women *or* young men; diminishing and imprisoning is more like it.

Most of the women I've heard from on the topic of hooking up seem a lot less likely to want to shout "I am woman; hear me roar!" during a casual sexual encounter than to murmur reassuringly to themselves, "This is okay, right? This is cool. This is what people do, isn't it?"

Among the more surprising aspects of the college hookup culture to me was the students' awareness that hooking up was about a code of behavior and a set of rules they had to follow, yet hardly anyone seemed to know exactly what those rules entailed. Though they generally assumed it involved a carefree attitude about having physical relationships without commitment, beyond that the rules escaped them. Did you have to have sex for it to be a hookup? Or just be intimate somehow? Hard to know for sure. And hard to get answers by asking around, lest you reveal your ignorance. It's not as though the colleges had posted hookup guidelines in the dormitory hallways during freshmen orientation.

The one unifying theme, though, was a mutually agreed-to lack of emotional vulnerability. Whatever you did or felt, you had to remain aloof. Because once you revealed your vulnerability (or encountered vulnerability in someone else), there was the potential for conflict and mess. Though also, of course, for connection and beauty. That was the rub. And the risk.

The first time I held the college essay contest, in 2008, hooking up was the hot topic, something hundreds of students chose to explore. When I reprised the contest three years later, hooking up was still widely practiced but no longer of interest in terms of what students were trying to figure out. I don't know if they believed they had figured it out or if they had just decided to move on.

Whatever the case, the pendulum of their curiosity had swung 180 degrees in the other direction, from relationships that were meant to be strictly physical with no emotional component to those that were strictly emotional with no physical component. Meaning that it had become normalized for students to have their primary romantic relationship—the one that made their hearts pound, the one they spent hours every day obsessing over—be one that was conducted exclusively online, where they avoided the messiness of physical sexuality altogether while maintaining an emotional connection within the confines of a glowing (often handheld) screen.

Both behaviors—hooking up and conducting an exclusively online relationship—strike me as being primarily about self-protection and invulnerability, even if those participating in the online relationships believe they are pouring their hearts out into their Gchat boxes and laptop cams. It often seems like they are only freed up to do so because they aren't physically together and therefore can instantly end things with the click of a mouse.

EMBRACING VULNERABILITY: FROM "I LOVE YOU" TO THE GRAND GESTURE

AS POPULAR AS acting aloof may currently be, it's fair to say we're also in the midst of a vulnerability heyday, with hordes of people confessing every private detail of their insecurities and desires, neither inhibited about doing so nor fearful of consequences. The Modern Love column, by virtue of appearing in the highest-circulation Sunday newspaper in the country, obviously has a large potential audience in print. And the *New York Times* website has extended that readership to every corner of the world. If you're skittish about exposing your vulnerability to strangers, confessing the details of your love life in such a well-read venue might be considered a scary proposition.

In the column's early years, that may have held true for certain people and certain subjects. The transgender experience, for example, with sexual reassignment surgery and all of the complexity such a change entails and the confusion it often sows, is a subject that could make a lot of people uncomfortable, and airing one's personal story about it might feel prohibitively risky. For whatever reason, almost no one—if anyone—broached the topic among the thousands of stories I received. Eventually I found an essay on the subject by the pioneering transgender writer Jennifer Finney Boylan in an anthology that was soon to be published, and I was able to adapt her wonderful piece for the column. In the first five years, that's all I could muster in terms of opening a window into this fascinating and wrenching experience.

And then the floodgates opened, and I was receiving dozens of the most intimate essays on that topic imaginable, from every angle—wives, girlfriends, and sisters of those going through the change—until we had reached the point where we had to pull back because we'd covered it so much. Any sense of taboo or self-censorship had vanished. In fact, the notion of "taboo" seems to be in steady retreat in the twenty-first century, at least from where I sit. When it comes to revealing personal secrets and predilections, so many people are emerging from so many different closets you can hardly keep track of who was originally behind what.

Another cautionary note: Not all displays of vulnerability are effective or even genuine. Some people share their anxieties and private shames immediately and indiscriminately, but vulnerability is more credible and effective when it's rationed out and offered with humility, not sprayed scattershot. So while acting vulnerable is generally good, try not to go off the deep end with it. Vulnerability, like anything else, can be done either deeply or shallowly.

Being the First to Say "I Love You"

Everyone knows that just because you realize you're falling in love with someone doesn't mean you're supposed to blurt that out until you've gotten a good sense that your declaration of love will be reciprocated. If you think of your relationship as being like a seesaw, with you on one end and your love interest on the other, then you want to try to keep that seesaw roughly in balance and avoid any sudden shifts that can result in a sharp fall and a broken ass.

For example, if you say "I love you," and the other person says "I love you too," the seesaw remains balanced. But if you say "I love you," and he or she pauses and then says, "Um, I really like you a lot, but—" it's as if your seesaw partner has stood up and let you go crashing down.

The big decision, though, is figuring out who is going to be the first to say "I love you." Well, it turns out there's some consistency in this matter, at least in heterosexual relationships. Researchers at Penn State University have found that men are actually three times more likely than women to be the first in the relationship to say "I love you." Surprised? I was, and so were the 87 percent of people in the study who expected women would be the first to profess love. The logic comes clear, though, when you understand the timing and reasons why men are often the first to cross that threshold.

According to the study, men typically say "I love you" *before* they have had sex with the woman, and the reason they decide to say it, consciously or not, is because they want to have sex, and they think the woman is more likely to agree to have sex if she is told she's loved.

Although this makes sense, I doubt it's so coldly calculated in every case, because from what I've seen (and done), a man's brain can confuse intense physical desire with actual love, and in the heat of the moment, he may not be able to process his feelings and thoughts appropriately. In these cases, his brain may seize up, and before he even knows what's happening, his mouth just spits out the words "I love you." He sort of means it but also sort of can't help himself.

In any case, if it works, and the man gets to have sex, he's happy, even if he hasn't quite thought through the long-term repercussions of how the woman may interpret his declaration and what she will hold him to going forward and how often she will remind him of it.

The Unintentional Admission

One added twist to the "I love you" scenario involves the unintentional admission. This occurs when one person in a relationship thinks the other has said "I love you," so he or she then responds by saying "I love you too." (Note: those who are in a romantic relationship with someone who mumbles a lot, talks fast and/or monotonously, and/or speaks with a heavy foreign accent are especially at risk of being lured into making an unintentional admission.)

You'll know instantly when you've stumbled into such a situation, because after you say "I love you too," the other person may look at you with a strange expression, grin nervously, and then ask, "What did you think I just said?"

As the blood drains from your face, you manage to squeak out, "I thought you said, 'I love you.'"

Your partner may then laugh and say something like: "I didn't say 'I love you.' I said, 'I love stew.' You know, the really good beef stew they have in the cafeteria?"

Or: "I love Stu. You know, that guy who always gets us the great theater tickets?"

Or: "I love dew. You know, the way it sparkles in the grass? It looks kind of magical, don't you think?"

Whatever the case, your hand got played. You were tricked into laying down your cards prematurely. You didn't intend to be the first to say "I love you," even if that's how you felt, but now you've gone ahead and done it. The good news: more often than not, the unintentional admission seems to lead to a happy result. If you were that quick on the draw, chances are your love had been an unspoken truth in the relationship for some time and you'd been itching to come clean about it. And now, depending on the response, you'll finally know if you should move forward or move on. Either way, you're probably better off.

I've seen other variations of the unintentional admission. All the recent momentum toward legalizing gay marriage had made a partner in one lesbian couple start wondering about marriage. She secretly wanted to get married but was afraid to say so because her partner had spoken so dismissively about it.

But was her partner against marriage in general, as some heteronormative sham of an institution to which she'd never want to belong? Or was she against their marriage in particular and talking broadly about it as a way of sending a signal?

The woman who wanted to marry wasn't sure. So she had circled awkwardly around the topic, mostly acting as if the possibility still didn't really apply to them. Until one day, while they were having lunch at a café near the beach while vacationing in Florida, a low-flying plane drifted past pulling an advertising banner. In this case the ad was a proposal of marriage to a woman on the beach.

The partner who wanted to marry was the one facing the ocean. And when the plane flew by, she didn't catch the beginning of the message but started reading after the name, so her statement came out as halting and completely out of context. "Will you marry me—" she said uncertainly, followed by a pause.

At which point her partner, who was unaware of the plane and its banner, abruptly stopped eating, gazed up misty-eyed from her plate, and answered, "Yes."

The misfire was soon explained. But after laughing at the fumbled exchange, they realized that an accepted marriage proposal had been floated between them—the desire and vulnerability had been exposed—and it had to be dealt with one way or another.

Seriously? they each thought.

Yes, seriously.

So not long after, as soon as their state decided to allow same-sex couples to marry, that's exactly what they did.

The Grand Gesture (Hint: You Must Travel to Beijing)
Everyone loves to hear stories about a grand gesture, yet few are truly willing to do what it takes to pull one off. First, what even

is a grand gesture? Let's begin by talking about what a grand gesture is not.

A grand gesture is not something you film for YouTube. If you have set up high-definition cameras at various angles and brought in a soundman and maybe even choreographed a flash mob of friends to accompany your surprise declaration of affection or proposal of marriage, you are probably more interested in how many video views you can get than in true acts of vulnerability.

A grand gesture is not a gaudy gift. Gaudy gifts tend to be more about power plays and bribery.

A grand gesture is not an act that will humiliate anyone else. It may humiliate you but not the object of your affection. This rules out hiring a plane or a blimp to tow an I LOVE YOU, CARLA sign over a stadium at which you are attending a major-league sporting event. Arranging to broadcast your message at halftime on the stadium's Jumbotron as the announcer blares out your names to seventy thousand people isn't it either.

The grand gestures I'm talking about are quiet acts of extreme vulnerability and bravery. Your only audience is the person you're pursuing. The only gaudiness is how outsized your act is compared to what most people are willing to risk for love.

Ideally, the beneficiary of your gesture will not feel embarrassed by your act but deeply flattered. In a true grand gesture, you don't know the outcome. You don't know whether your feelings will be reciprocated. You are taking a huge risk.

Oddly, though, in a real grand gesture you don't tend to pity the person if he or she is rebuffed. The fact that they were able to lay themselves that far out for love means they're probably going to be just fine in the world. If anything, you're more likely to feel astonishment, admiration, and even envy at their bravery.

So why can't more of us step up to the plate? Because we're afraid that doing so will require us to be excruciatingly vulnerable in a way that will crush us and invite ridicule if we fail. And the sheer romanticism required can feel antiquated in this age of cynicism and self-protection.

The other reason more of us don't do it? Time and money. Often the grand gesture will require expensive long-distance travel and lodging. In fact, you'll probably have to fly to Beijing. I've published three bona fide grand gesture stories in nine years, and all three involved traveling to Beijing. What's the deal with Beijing? I have no idea. I would have thought Paris or Rome or Rio, but no. Apparently one other thing we've begun outsourcing to China is romance.

In the first story, Lisa was a freshman in college when she fell hard for a female poet—a flighty, whip-smart upperclassman who had a boyfriend and lived in a castle-like building off campus. They became close friends, but not lovers, and Lisa was devastated many months later when the object of her affection abruptly announced she was moving to Japan.

Stung by the news yet undeterred, Lisa plotted to apply for foreign study in Japan the next year, for no other reason than to reunite with her friend and confess her love once and for all. When Japan turned out not to be economically feasible for her, she learned at the foreign study office that there was a summer program in Beijing she could apply for.

Beijing, she decided, would have to be close enough.

By June she was studying Mandarin at Peking University on an open-jaw airline ticket. Six weeks later the program ended, and her friend came from Japan to join her in Tiananmen Square, where they flew kites together. It was, to Lisa, nothing short of magical. Her friend wanted to take the Trans-Siberian Railway through Russia and then wing it from there. Did Lisa want to join her?

She did!

While traveling together, Lisa's desire finally boiled to the surface one night, and they kissed. Yet Lisa's love for her friend, while not spurned, was not fully reciprocated either. Her friend remained emotionally elusive. And ultimately, Lisa just couldn't keep up. She had to go back home to her real life. But she didn't regret her leap. She had traveled and loved and learned. Her grand gesture had proven to be the greatest adventure of her life.

Ellen also took an around-the-world leap, yet hers was into the total unknown. Divorced at forty-six, Ellen was living alone in upstate New York when her Chinese friend Yuhzi expressed one day that she was concerned. She worried that Ellen was lonely. Yuhzi had a brother in China, Zhong-Hua, who was lonely, too. Maybe they would like each other?

She offered to help send Ellen to China to find out. "But if you don't like him, is okay," she added.

Much to her own surprise, Ellen accepted.

Four months later, she disembarked her plane at the Beijing airport and approached a man in baggage claim who was holding a bouquet of red roses. Zhong-Hua spoke and understood almost no English. Ellen spoke and understood almost no Mandarin. But she liked him, or at least was open to him. And it meant a lot to her that he, sight unseen, was open to her, too. Other kinds of more traditional and less risky love had failed her. She had been burned by divorce. So why not try this?

They spent three weeks together, a period during which they were barely able to communicate but enjoyed each other's company nevertheless. When Zhong-Hua proposed to Ellen near the end of her stay—"Do you want marry?" he asked—she surprised herself again by saying yes. His proposal was the only complete sentence of English he'd managed to learn, and she couldn't believe he had mastered it.

She went back home shortly thereafter, and together they then had to wait eighteen months for his visa to be approved before he could move to the US. During this time they communicated as best they could, with Zhong-Hua devoting several days to crafting each short letter to her in English, writing sentiments like: "In my imagination, I see your slim figure buffeted by icy gusts of wind, and I want to cross the street and stand next to you. I long to shield you from the cold."

Finally, he was allowed to come to the US and join Ellen in her upstate New York home. During the long winters there, he was able to shield her from the cold, just as he'd once imagined. And many years later, he still is.

The Aloof Grand Gesture

This may be the most intriguing category of all. In performing an aloof grand gesture, you go to great expense and trouble to connect with someone you think you might love, but you never admit to the object of your affection that the expense and trouble was about him or her. The whole time you must act aloof, as if you have done nothing special. A textbook case, also involving a trip to Beijing (where else?), crossed my desk several years ago.

Kim was working as a producer for a television show in New York when a journalist who was an American correspondent in Beijing appeared as a guest. She saw the man on the monitor during the interview segment and was intrigued by him, but they didn't actually meet in person. Her colleague, though, who was the booking agent for the show, told the man afterward that he and the producer on the show, Kim, might hit it off.

Embarrassed at learning what her colleague had done, Kim e-mailed the man a breezy but apologetic message, saying: "Sorry my coworker is being so presumptuous. Just ignore her attempts at matchmaking." She added a joke about blind dates being a standard parting gift for guests of the show.

This launched an e-mail exchange between them in which they began sharing all kinds of personal history, peppering each other with questions and updates on their lives. As the months passed, though, it seemed to Kim that she was revealing more than he was. This dynamic, combined with her otherwise lack-luster love life, led Kim to idealize him even more. The less he told her about himself, the more she filled in the blanks with a fantasized vision of him and of what they might be together.

While reading a travel magazine about Asia, she got inspired and decided to make her move. She would travel to Beijing and see him. To spare herself the embarrassment and to relieve any pressure on him, she would let him know she was coming for some invented reason—a freelance writing assignment!—and simply ask if he wanted to get together while she was there.

Three thousand dollars and two days of travel later, there they were, in person, having dinner together in a bright, sterile restaurant, where her fantasy was replaced by something real if uncertain. They liked each other, they spoke warmly, they went from dinner to a bar where they met up with some friends of his, and at the end of the evening he kissed her on the cheek and asked to see her again.

The next few evenings they spoke on the phone, with her having to lie each time about the work she'd been doing all day on her fake freelance writing assignment, when in fact she had zero responsibilities and was merely sightseeing. On her last night they again met for dinner, after which they went back to his apartment, where they talked for hours into the night.

Around one thirty A.M., just when she was thinking the date might take a turn toward the physical, a transition that almost certainly would have led her to confess to her grand gesture (coming clean about the insanity of it but also embracing it as one of the best decisions she'd ever made), it was he who had a confession to make. He'd recently begun a relationship with another woman, he told her, a relationship he felt had potential.

His confession usurped hers; she kept her secret to herself. Blabbing it out at that point probably would have made them both feel awkward. In any case, she flew back home the next day as alone as she'd come, but with the knowledge of her experience and a sense of closure that she appreciated.

And there was this, too: she realized that he hadn't told her about the other woman during their two dinners together, although at that point it already had been a monthlong relationship. He had seemed to be open to her, in fact, showing her affection and warmth during their dates. Which meant to Kim that he had taken a small leap, too, wondering whether something was possible with her. Not as big a leap as hers, surely, but a leap nonetheless. And that counted.

But Kim's story didn't end there; she decided to write up an essay about the experience over the following months, and she sent that essay to me. And I chose to have it appear in the newspaper. As part of our editorial process, we asked Kim to inform her Beijing heartthrob about the story, revealing to him the truth about her gesture and what actually had transpired between them years earlier. And he congratulated her. Warmly!

So warmly that he and Kim ended up professing their mutual love, marrying, and living happily ever after?

No, not that warmly. Life already had moved on for both of them. And Kim will never know if her coming clean at the time, during their last night together in Beijing, might have made a difference. That's the trade-off with the aloof grand gesture: you get to keep your pride, but you never find out if you might have been able to keep something else instead.

WEARING ARMOR: FROM SINGLE GIRL'S STARTER KITS TO MODIFIED WEDDING VOWS

HEADING OFF INTO the field of relationships while wearing emotional armor may be the most popular choice of the three. After all, few choose to remain on the sidelines forever, and fewer still are able to stride out into that field totally exposed. Nearly all of us hedge our bets to some degree. Here are a couple of ways hedging (and overcoming hedging) can play out in a relationship.

Single Girl's Starter Kit (Also Comes in a Male Version, Presumably)

Julia loved her boyfriend. She trusted her boyfriend. Her boyfriend made her oatmeal and brought it to her in bed. He brought her coffee. He cherished her and was perfect for her.

Nevertheless, Julia felt she had to plan for love's end. Ever since her heroes Sonny and Cher broke up, shattering her childhood image of love's reliability, she had learned that love came and love went and you'd better be prepared for when it went. If the couple who sang "I Got You Babe" every week to millions while gazing lovingly at each other could call it quits, then anyone could—and probably would.

And in her life they had. Her grandfather left her grandmother to join the circus (seriously). Her father left her mother for another woman while in the throes of a midlife crisis. Men left. Love didn't last. As an adult, Julia endured the unraveling of several of her own relationships, leaving her devastated in different ways.

So even though she lived with her boyfriend and loved her boyfriend, she also maintained a secret escape hatch in case it all got ripped out from underneath her. She paid $189 a month for a rented storage space in which she kept her Single Girl's Starter Kit—everything she would need if she and her boyfriend ever were to break up. Granted, the Starter Kit was mostly psychological. Of course she couldn't account for every need. But the essentials were there: bed, sheets, pillow, an afghan, kitchen utensils, tool kit, ladder, and a box of love letters from past admirers.

Her friends warned her that by preparing for a relationship's end at the beginning, she was ensuring its demise. They argued that her Single Girl's Starter Kit could prove to be a self-fulfilling prophecy.

Maybe. But she still wasn't giving it up. It was her armor. She even thought of it as her romantic bomb shelter, a place to protect her from harm. One more thing: She had kept the existence of the Single Girl's Starter Kit a secret from her boyfriend. He knew she had a storage unit, but she'd implied it contained boxes of tax records and old clothing she hoped to fit into again someday. Why tell him about its true contents and significance if knowing about her caution and backup plan might hurt him? He was a widower, after all. His life had fallen apart after his wife died. He was well acquainted with loss. With his wife, he'd been all in, and look where that had gotten him. Julia couldn't imagine ever being all in.

And then their landlord threatened to double their rent. This made the cost of her storage unit even harder to defend. So finally she decided to tell her boyfriend about it. She confessed to him the contents of the unit and their purpose.

Thankfully, he wasn't hurt. He even understood. "My late wife had one," he said, explaining that she had paid rent on an unoccupied studio apartment for the first two years of their relationship.

And this made Julia feel better about keeping it. Oddly, though, the kindness and understanding of his response also made her feel better about possibly getting rid of it. Of finally going all in. Yes, she decided, maybe she would. After all, her boyfriend was never going to run off and join the circus. And neither was she.

Modified Wedding Vows

I don't win very many arguments with my wife, but I prevailed on this one: In planning our wedding, Cathi wanted to edit our wedding vows to better reflect (in her view) the reality of contemporary marriage. I actually agreed with the rationale for her suggested changes—they would have better reflected marriage's reality—but I feared that if we were to stand up and say them her way in front of 120 of our (and our parents') nearest and dearest while slipping rings on each other's fingers, people would laugh at us.

Weddings are generous events and may include a lot of quirky personal touches that lighten up the occasion, but being laughed at (not with) by all the people you love and respect while reading your vows shouldn't be one of them. Or so I argued.

Here's my vague memory of the vows we planned to say, with the additions Cathi had sought italicized:

"I promise to *try my best to* remain faithful from this day forward, to *try my best to* take care of you in sickness and in health, and to *try my best to* . . ."

You get the idea. Cathi thought the idea of vowing something you might not be able to follow through on was dishonest at best. She thought saying words in a certain way just because billions of other people had said them that way was shallow and stupid. She also thought throwing your bouquet into a crowd of shrieking single women was sexist and insulting and ridiculous and she didn't want to do it. She thought smashing cake into each other's faces as everyone clapped and cheered was disgusting and wasteful; she loves cake (it's basically her favorite food), and she wanted to be able to sit down and enjoy her cake like a normal person, not have it smeared ear to ear as if she were some drunken frat boy.

Our wedding, in her view, should be how we wanted it because it was going to be our "special day." (Or at least that's the phrase our photographer kept repeating—"This is your special day!"—as he tried to sell us the expensive leather-bound book over the chintzy Naugahyde version that came with the package, a tactic we totally fell for, of course.)

For Cathi, our special day would be more special if we simply made a few sensible changes to the program. It wasn't much in the way of armor, but it was armor nonetheless. She had typical fears about marriage and this was one way of dealing with them. And also the editor in her knew that those traditional vows, musty from decades of neglect, were begging for someone with a red pen.

"How many people cheat in marriage after saying those vows?" she asked. "How many people walk out on their husband or wife when things get hard?" She said she loved me—for the time being, anyway—but she didn't want to overpromise.

In the end, though, in one of her rare concessions, our vows remained as traditional vows, and we both overpromised. She promised all those things to me without qualification, and I promised them all back to her without qualification, and we've been "trying our best" to honor them in marriage ever since.

So far, so good.

4

Connection

I LUV U JUST THE WAY U R

WHEN I WAS IN MIDDLE SCHOOL, my older brother got a Pet Rock for Christmas. Pet Rocks were the big gift that year. Packaged in a little cardboard box (with air holes), the Pet Rock came with an instruction booklet that showed you how to care for it—the obvious joke being that it required no care. The rock itself was the kind of well-worn stone you might find on a New England beach, oblong and smooth. No attempt had been made to give it a face or bodily features or to make it look in any way like a living creature. For $3.95 what you basically got was the rock, the booklet, and the packaging. The guy who came up with the idea, an advertising executive named Gary Dahl, quickly sold more than a million Pet Rocks and got filthy rich.

My high-school-aged brother already had a girlfriend to occupy him and didn't care about the Pet Rock, but I loved it. Every time I opened the box and saw the rock sitting in its bed of straw, I actually felt an emotional pull. There was something so vulnerable and compliant about the rock waiting in its little box all day, available to have a relationship with me whenever I wanted to have one but otherwise demanding nothing, not food or water or even oxygen, despite its air holes. I wasn't ready for a real relationship anyway, so this was perfect, at least for as long as our fling lasted, which was about two weeks.

When I was feeling especially needy and sentimental I even could pretend the rock missed me when I was at school and was happy to see me when I returned. And when I grew bored of the rock's company (which happened almost immediately), I could put it away, return the box to my brother's shelf, and not have to care about it anymore.

I hadn't thought about my brother's Pet Rock in decades, until recently when I was reminded of that special relationship from my childhood while reading another saga of someone's online-only relationship. Not to insult any online lovers with the comparison—I realize there are huge differences between having an online relationship with a human being and an in-person relationship with a rock. For starters, rocks have no emotional life (that we know of), so they won't lash out or guilt-trip you if you neglect them. But there are plenty of other notable differences as well, like the fact that rocks can't think, tell jokes, laugh, understand irony, share stories from their past, talk dirty, register for a Skype account, open a laptop, work a mouse, disrobe in front of a laptop camera, or masturbate—all popular activities of online relationships between human beings.

Even so, I'm often struck by the "Pet Rock" quality of many online-only relationships, which tend to thrive—as do so many online activities—from the same combination of fantasy, convenience, and control that fueled my brief affair with my brother's rock. What's more, they especially seem to appeal to people who aren't ready for, can't find, or don't want a real relationship, so having an intense connection via words and a screen is perfect, at least for as long as the fling lasts, which in some cases can be years.

First, let me clarify: By saying "online-only relationship," I'm not talking about a couple who happen to be temporarily separated by school, a job, a travel assignment, or military service and is maintaining contact via the Web until they can be reunited. Nor am I talking about high school or college sweethearts who find each other on Facebook years later and start an instant-message or Skype flirtation. What I'm talking about are people who met online (or perhaps just briefly in person) and whose only way of getting to know each other is by e-mailing, texting, e-chatting, blogging, tweeting, and Skyping.

These relationships are exploding in popularity. This is love's new frontier, romance that is travel-ready and designed to fit in the palm of your hand. No risky sex. No slamming of doors or underwear on the floor or dirty dishes in the sink. No pestering for a back massage or pushiness about how if you like it then you should really "put a ring on it." Just a deep emotional bond with a twenty-first-century pen pal with whom you can remain in more or less constant contact and to whom you can pour out your every waking thought and emotion. The actual dollar cost of such relationships typically hovers around zero. The emotional investment, however, tends to be somewhat higher.

SOUL MATE IN A BOX

ONLINE-ONLY RELATIONSHIPS are incredibly easy to start. Maybe too easy. You probably already have everything you need—a WiFi-enabled device, a data plan, and a burning sense of unfulfilled desire. Before long you too can be enjoying nearly unlimited access to an on-screen personality who gets you on every level, a virtual "Soul Mate in a Box." It's hard to say where exactly you might locate your Soul Mate in a Box (SMIAB, for short), but in general they aren't very hard to find. Potential SMIABs lurk in practically every social media platform you might access.

Maybe yours will first appear as a commenter on a friend's Facebook post, delivering some witty aside accompanied by a sexy profile pic, prompting you to investigate who this alluring creature might be. So you start clicking on links, scouring through photo albums, mining personal data, growing more titillated by the moment. Within minutes you may enter full fantasy mode, and pretty soon you're trying to think of some way to reach out and connect to this dream doll or dude that wouldn't be considered overly stalkerish. Liking their comment, perhaps? Commenting on their comment? Being really bold and sending a friend request? The possibilities are thrilling.

Where you find your SMIAB ultimately depends, of course, on where you tend to hang out online. If Twitter is your thing, and you've tweeted and retweeted entertainingly enough to collect a following that goes beyond friends and family, then you've surely experienced the special ego boost that can come from seeing that some fellow tweeter has decided, out of the blue, to follow you. Makes you feel kind of intelligent and sexy when that happens, doesn't it? The same minor but not insignificant ego boost can occur when a stranger "likes" a comment you've made on a blog or a Facebook post, or, better yet, decides to comment on your comment in a flattering way.

This random admiration can feel like the equivalent of a stranger coming up behind you in a bar, tapping you on the shoulder, and saying, "Sorry, but I couldn't help overhearing what you were saying just now, and I just wanted to tell you how brilliant and funny I thought it was. I could listen to you all day and night. In fact, would you mind if I just sat next to you on this stool and waited for you to make smart and witty remarks?"

How often has that happened to you in a bar? Never. It has never happened to anyone in a bar. Yet online it's happening to someone every second of every day—so much vague flattery so freely dispensed. If you're feeling unappreciated in your regular life (and really, who isn't?), this kind of attention can be all it takes to ignite an online relationship. However the relationship then rolls out, from a first encounter in a chat room or through a flurry of flirtatious tweets, blog comments, or Facebook messaging, the thing can rapidly catch fire, accelerated by the feeling that this is just breezy fun with little if any risk. After all, you're probably separated by many miles or mountain ranges or possibly even continents or oceans. You may be further walled off by existing relationships and commitments, by spouses and children.

You're never going to actually meet each other in the flesh or even speak on the phone, or so you tell yourself. It's never going to mean anything. This shared understanding is what allows you to *act* vulnerable without actually having to *feel* vulnerable.

(In this respect, an online-only relationship is the polar opposite of the hookup, where people complain they often *feel* vulnerable but aren't allowed to *act* vulnerable.)

You keep up the banter because it's so fun and liberating, and soon your mutual admiration-fest snowballs into an ever deeper and more fulfilling connection, until not only does the relationship mean something to you—it means everything. It has become the one relationship you think about all the time.

Part of the appeal of online-only relationships is convenience. They can be shoehorned into the participants' daily lives wherever and whenever they want: at work in an open chat window next to the legal brief they're writing or by a constant exchange of text messages from home, car, bike, or beach. But the greater allure, the virtue of which I hear people rave about again and again, is the intensity of the connection—to someone they've never met or spoken to in real life—which has reached a deeper level than anything they've experienced during any in-person relationship they've ever had.

TAKING GREATER RISKS FROM A SAFE PLACE

SOME MAINTAIN THAT the intensity occurs not despite the fact that they've never met but *because* they haven't. It's as if the stripping away of the physical awkwardness and expectations has freed the online lovers to mainline each other's personalities like heroin: insert needle, meld hearts and minds. They believe what they have together exists on a higher and purer plane because it's unsullied by all those in-person downers like small talk, petty disagreements, and disappointing sexual experiences.

Those who don't yet want or have monogamous, long-term relationships can actually use the limitations of hookups and SMIABs to their advantage by taking an à la carte approach to their love lives and combining regular hookups with a SMIAB. That way they can get their physical needs met locally and their emotional needs met distantly without having to worry that either dalliance will grow into the real relationship they either fear or simply don't yet want. By ordering up each kind of relationship as a side dish rather than a full meal, they can preserve their essential singlehood until they're ready for more.

Many participating in online-only relationships openly fear any attempt to turn what they have into something more. After all, they luv u the way u r and don't really want 2 find out who u might b in person. This skittishness infects all age groups: the committed mid-lifers don't want their online flirtation to blossom into something that threatens to derail their settled lives, while the young and unattached don't want it to blossom into something that threatens to derail their *un*settled lives.

Yet it's hard to keep the genie in the bottle, or, in this case, on the other side of the screen. Such affairs can't seem to stay contained in that perfect place no matter how much the participants want them to. Which brings me to yet another significant difference between having a relationship with a Soul Mate in a Box versus having a relationship with a rock in a box: a rock can't get out of its box by itself, whereas a SMIAB not only can but almost certainly will.

As Woody Allen famously observed in *Annie Hall*: "A relationship is like a shark, you know? It has to constantly move forward or it dies." With online affairs, the only way to move the relationship forward after a certain point or passage of time is to agree to meet in person. And when you decide to make this leap, the relationship that began with no pressure and zero expectations suddenly can carry the weight of the world. Whether it's weeks or months or years of online communication, the questions that precede a face-to-face meeting are always the same: Will we even like each other in person? Will he/she find me attractive and vice versa? Will we have the same chemistry that we do online?

They hope they will but suspect they won't. They've already heard about how these things go. Yet meet they must. Move forward or die, right? Or, as commonly happens when SMIABs arrange to meet in person, move forward *and* die, since so few seem to successfully transition from an online relationship to one that works in real life. Most often, couples who get together after months or years of online infatuation enact a twenty-first-century version of Icarus flying too close to the sun with his waxen wings: the real-life exposure quickly melts the fiber-optic cable that was holding the couple aloft, and they plummet into the sea, where they tend to flail about for a while, trying to rescue their former magic.

It's hard to undo the damage from the fall. This instant implosion happens with stunning regularity. The mystery is why. If they had grown closer emotionally than they thought was possible with another human being, how could such closeness so suddenly evaporate?

IT'S ALL ABOUT THE DEVICE

FOR SOME IT appears that the relationship, and their whole way of growing close, was simply too wrapped up in the electronic device. Laptops and smartphones are changing our behavior and brains in ways we're just beginning to understand, but one change that seems all too clear is how the ease, control, and dazzling features of smartphones can make living our lives through them preferable to living in the physical world that surrounds us.

Let's look at the example of Caitlin, a college student whose intense online relationship began with a brief, unremarkable conversation with a guy in a loud hotel bar during a Web journalism conference they were both attending. After chatting for a few minutes about blogs and coding language, they said goodbye, with her joking that maybe she'd find him on Twitter.

Caitlin never thought they'd see each other again. After all, he lived three states and hundreds of miles away. Yet it wasn't long before she did find him on Twitter and began vaguely checking his feed every so often. Then one night when he'd been drinking, he sent her a provocative message via Gchat, and soon their Skype relationship began, a "Soul Mate in a Box" type of bond that quickly overtook their lives. They began video chatting for hours at a time and even would fall asleep with their laptops open, still connected via Skype, and awake to see the other musshaired and bleary-eyed, or still snoozing, legs twisted in cords.

They talked about everything, shared everything, and believed they were getting to know each other completely. Like a committed couple, they went to sleep together, awoke together, and relied on the existence of their relationship for emotional and intellectual sustenance throughout the day. With the camera, they even felt physically close. If he leaned near enough to the laptop cam, Caitlin remarked that she could see the pores on his face.

For her, the relationship felt intimate and nourishing yet perfectly controlled. She didn't have to see him in person or worry about that awkwardness, so she was never nervous, never hesitated to initiate contact or say whatever was on her mind. And she could click him off whenever she wanted to or not engage if she was busy. But if they got along this well and felt this close, shouldn't they meet in real life and test out their in-person compatibility, try to see if they had more than an online future together?

They agreed they should. So one Friday Caitlin rented a car, left school early, and drove for nine hours through three states to visit him for the weekend. In person, to her great relief, he seemed comfortably familiar, their initial meeting wasn't too weird, and she was hopeful. But before long it became clear that he wasn't acting as she expected he would, meaning he wasn't acting as he had on Skype.

The first sign of trouble was that he couldn't think of anything to say. He was perfectly nice, and so was she. But remarkably, this couple who couldn't get enough of each other online, who couldn't ask enough questions or wonder more about the details of each other's days and the trivialities of their thoughts, had suddenly lost nearly all curiosity about each other now that they were physically in the same room. In real life, they apparently weren't as interested or as interesting. And in this wondrous electronic age, that's often the case: the thing that's standing, sitting, or lying right next to us isn't as compelling as the thing on the screen. As these doubts crept in, so did their insecurities about who they were in person. Soon Caitlin was worrying she wasn't as physically attractive "live"—not as thin, for example, as she appeared on the screen.

Her insecurity began to feed on itself as her SMIAB's attention kept drifting from her to his phone and his laptop when they were out to dinner together or just hanging around his apartment. He was scanning the digital horizon as he'd always done, checking his Twitter feed and blog stats and following the lives of his other online "friends." After all, that's where he was used to getting his emotional fix.

Eventually it got to the point where Caitlin, wised up but heartbroken, accepted that their dynamic wasn't going to improve, and she decided to leave, though she could hardly blame him alone. The truth was, she couldn't think of anything to say either. By the end she couldn't even think of much to write. In her parting note, she was reduced to perfunctory small talk. "Thank you so much for having me this weekend," she wrote. "It meant a lot to me to spend time with you in person."

And that was the final telling difference: that a relationship founded on honesty, on sharing every emotional burp, would end with this kind of strained message. Because spending time with him in person was not something she felt grateful for. The entire trip had turned out to be dull, costly, and painful. Visiting him had ruined everything. Yet at the same time, what choice did they have? Never meeting? Staying glued to their screens and always wondering what might have been?

IT'S ALL ABOUT THE PERSONA

A WOMAN I heard from not long ago had been carrying on a racy online affair with some guy for months via text message and Gchat, talking about their fetishes and desires and all those fun and nasty things they wanted do to one another in person. Then they decided to upgrade their relationship to Skype. While they liked being able to see each other in the flesh—especially once they got naked in front of their laptop cams and *were* in the flesh—they felt weird talking to each other in their real voices, and they simply couldn't do it.

After the hundreds of hours they'd spent Gchatting, it turned out they had become too comfortable with their written personas to be able to communicate naturally by looking at each other and talking. They weren't self-conscious about stripping their clothes off and becoming physically naked, but they were self-conscious about speaking to each other without the filter of the keyboard. Why? Because they were different people when they were writing and speaking, and once they were able to compare, they preferred the written versions. So they decided to revert to using the chat boxes while looking silently at each other on the screen, communicating easily via typed messages as they always had.

Strange as it may seem, a lot of us are like that—we have one voice in writing and another voice in person. For example, in writing I'm apparently someone who begins sentences with throwaway phrases like "strange as it may seem," whereas if I were talking to someone at a party I would never say something like that. Nor, while speaking, would I ever use a word like "whereas." Nor would I ever begin two sentences in a row with "nor."

For some reason that's how I talk in a book. I don't know where it comes from—probably a mix of the voices in all the books I've digested over my lifetime. It's my author persona. Everyone has an author persona, but those who write more tend to have more developed author personas than those who write less. And those who write more are the kind of people who seek out and feel so liberated by online-only relationships, because they feel like they are their best selves in writing, and now they can let that best self shine in a relationship.

The problem is that this persona is just a part of us, not all of us. And in some ways it may actually be the opposite of who we are in person. Many are surprised by how bold, brash, and sexy they tend to be online when in person they are shy, retreating, and prudish. Yet the deeper we get with someone in an online-only relationship, the more we get tricked into believing our online persona is the real us. We really are that bold and funny and smart! At least we are with our SMIAB. He or she allows us to be our best self, which is exactly what love is supposed to do, right?

Then you meet him or her in person, or even just on Skype, and that charismatic self you've been nurturing and believing in all these months vanishes, replaced by the unfunny, inarticulate, wallflower version of yourself you thought you'd finally left behind. As it turned out, though, she'd just been temporarily shoved aside by your author persona. Here you are again, though, the quiet and fumbling you, making a surprise-guest appearance at the worst possible moment. Damn.

A SECOND LIFE THAT'S DISTRESSINGLY SIMILAR TO YOUR FIRST LIFE

TAKE HEART, THOUGH, because there may be another way to try to escape your worst and most embarrassing self. How? By turning yourself into a cartoon character that engages in relationships on your behalf. On Second Life (SecondLife.com), an online community anyone can join, you can experience relationships as an avatar in a video game. Your interactions are still on a screen, sanitized and anonymous, so you can shed your inhibitions. But it's also interactive, in that your avatar can get physical with other avatars, so it can feel a step beyond merely communicating with someone electronically.

On Second Life, the other cartoon characters your avatar encounters are designed and driven by the desires and decision making of other people just like you. So your avatar can work, shop, travel, build friendships, have enduring relationships, enjoy casual sex, hire prostitutes, explore your fetishes, and attempt to live however you want it to. Like any video game, though, you have to learn to master it.

If you're new to Second Life and eager to connect with someone else's avatar in a romantic way, getting out of your clothes can be a challenge if you're attempting it for the first time. And when you do finally strip them away (and the clothes of your cartoon partner, too), you might be shocked to find that your cartoon bodies have more in common with mannequins than human beings. Brace yourself for breasts without nipples and crotches that are as smooth as a Ken doll's.

Not to worry, though. You can buy all those sex organs (yes, with real money—PayPal and all major credit cards accepted) and learn how to affix and operate them. You might even feel like a giddy, fumbling teen again, trying to make sure you're humping your cartoon lover in the right arrangement (i.e., the one with the penis doing the thrusting instead of being thrust upon). You just have to be patient. Like anything, proficiency requires time and experience. And you can still communicate via chat boxes, so you don't have to deal with actually having to talk to anyone and reveal your physical nervousness and anxiety.

Second Life is a place for play and escapism. You can see what flying might feel like or explore a lush jungle without fear of being attacked by insects or crocodiles. But when it comes to relationships, it turns out that fantasy may not feel much different from reality. After all, we still are who we are and act as we do, and when we design and control an avatar, that creation is still ultimately tied to our same personality and social prowess. As at any get-together, you still have to be good company, saying (or typing) witty things and not acting like an idiot. And while you can give yourself big breasts or bulging muscles and act with a boldness you'd never attempt in person—and the novelty of that may thrill for a while—you don't really stand out because everyone can do that, so ultimately it's just as level (or unlevel) a playing field as real life.

And when someone walks away from your avatar to go have sex with someone else's avatar instead, the sting of rejection and betrayal can feel just as real (because, alas, it *is* real). As one woman who went to Second Life hoping for an escape from her string of failed in-person love affairs ruefully concluded, "I find that I act much as I do in real life, and my Second Life relationships tend to fail the same way my real-life relationships do."

It's difficult, in other words, to escape the essence of who you really are through superficial change. You might travel far and wide, either on the Internet or by crossing physical borders, but in the end, as the saying goes: "Wherever you go, there you are."

Or as the saying may apply in the world of Second Life: "However big you make your avatar's penis, there you are."

WHEN ONLINE-ONLY IS THE ONLY WAY THAT WORKS

IF YOU'RE TRYING to move a relationship forward and get to know someone better, online-only has its limitations. But what if you already know the person too well and want to move the relationship backward to a safer place? In this case, online-only can be a salvation.

In Heather's case, her relationship with her father had been difficult for as long as she could remember. In her childhood he had been a drinker, a smoker, a philanderer, and prone to violence. He neglected his family and children, missed Heather's birthdays and her wedding, and blew his money on drifters and prostitutes. By the time Heather had reached her thirties, she thought, *This relationship might just be too hard.* Every time she saw him she regretted it. So she broke off contact, orchestrating certain necessities from afar but otherwise washing her hands of him.

Yet the separation weighed on her as any family estrangement would. Suddenly her father was eighty years old and in a nursing home, having suffered a stroke. She hadn't seen or spoken to him in years. And she probably wouldn't have if the nurse who was caring for him hadn't contacted Heather, asking if they could connect via Skype.

Heather was nervous about it. Her feelings about her father were complicated but at least somewhat contained, and she didn't know how this reopening of the past might play out. But now that her father was essentially defanged, lying harmless in a nursing-home bed unable to hurt anyone else or himself, she felt the compassion for him rush back. She didn't want to rush to his bedside, but she felt she could manage connecting via Skype.

So they did. They kept each other company, face-to-face, for long sessions every Friday until his death several months later. During those months, Skype gave Heather a safe way into a relationship she'd never had with her father. As Heather put it, "Here, in a box, was a man I could love."

Their time together didn't erase or replace the earlier memories but added a more nuanced picture of who he was and allowed her to know him and better come to terms with her own twisted emotions. Crucially, the connection allowed her to feel some measure of peace with him before he died.

I have heard similar stories from others in finding a way to connect with difficult or abusive parents, people grateful to be given an opportunity for forgiveness and grace that didn't used to be possible. An in-person encounter would be too fraught and a phone call too limiting and difficult. But real-time electronic communication gives them the chance to reconstruct relationships while feeling safe emotionally.

As expansive and liberating as online-only relationships can feel, they are as narrow as the cable that allows them to exist, and this narrowness can be like a tight-fitting sleeve that keeps the thing from busting out into something more. For some relationships, though, narrow is good. Narrow, in fact, can be everything.

5

Trust

LOVE'S NECESSARY GULLIBILITY

HAVE YOU EVER PARTICIPATED IN ONE of those trust exercises where you are told to stand on a platform, close your eyes, and fall backward into the arms of your colleagues or teammates or whomever it is you're supposed to be bonding with? Me neither. But I can appreciate the lesson. We learn to trust people by trusting people. We can't know our colleagues are going to catch us—we simply have to trust that they will.

Besides, what are the options? Refuse to participate and come off looking like some paranoid, antisocial freak when the whole point of the exercise is to establish trust and build camaraderie?

No. Whether we are attempting to fall backward off a platform or fall blindly in love, we need to approach the task with a basic faith in humanity. We need to believe that most people we encounter in our daily lives aren't out to harm us and may even try to save us if necessary. It might be to our advantage to act openly suspicious in certain situations, like if we're thinking about buying a Rolex watch from someone who is selling them on the street for twenty-five dollars apiece. But if we bring that level of wariness to our search for love, we risk looking damaged instead.

After all, love is for the sucker in us, not the skeptic. Love appeals to our gullible side, the part of us that wants to believe. Yet when we embrace our "inner sucker" and decide to trust, we also open ourselves up to being lied to, victimized, and hurt—not just by con artists and criminals looking to swindle us out of our life savings but by anyone who might act like they love us only to realize later that they don't.

In romance and seduction there always have been liars eager to take advantage of love's necessary gullibility for fun or profit, but in the past we were less exposed to this risk because we were more likely to date people we knew or had met through someone we knew. Except for organized singles events at bars or social clubs, where nearly everyone in attendance was local, romantic encounters with total strangers tended to be accidental, random, and infrequent. And when it came to falling in love with someone we'd never met or spoken to—well, that was virtually unheard of.

Today, though, we fall in love with someone we've never met or spoken to all the time. A passionate exchange of images and messages may be all it takes to turn a digital flirtation into our "everything." And for tens of millions, going out with total strangers we've met online—people with whom we have no connection whatsoever—has become a way of life.

Given how often we're flying blind these days in pursuing love, it's no surprise there's so much wariness among those in the hunt. As a way of defusing this fear, and perhaps to reassure our friends that we're not naïve about the risks, many of us like to joke about worst-case scenarios before heading out to meet a date for the first time, typically by uttering some version of the line "For all I know, he/she could be a _____ ."

How would you fill in the blank?

If you're like my fifty thousand strangers, you will probably say, in order of popularity, "axe murderer," "serial killer," or "total psycho." (Women tend to obsess about axe murderers and serial killers, while men are more inclined to fear total psychos.)

And sure, there's a chance, however remote, that you'll end up on a date with an axe murderer, a serial killer, or a total psycho. And maybe an air conditioner will fall on your head as you leave the restaurant. Or a meteor will strike your car on the way there. Or the Olive Garden will explode in a giant fireball just as your complimentary bread sticks arrive.

You can worry about anything, but worrying about getting paired up with an axe murderer shouldn't rank very high on your list. If you're truly concerned about this, however, OkCupid provides an "Are You an Axe Murderer?" quiz that evaluates a subscriber's propensity for axe murdering based on how he or she responds to a series of supposedly relevant questions. (Hint: if you want to avoid raising suspicion, don't answer that you like your French fries to be splattered with lots of ketchup.)

The head-scratching aspect of this quiz, though, is you only find out if *you* might be an axe murderer, not the person you're about to go out with. Maybe the hope is that potential axe murderers, once they digest their quiz results and acknowledge their capacity for violence, will responsibly remove themselves from the dating pool?

If every axe murderer were to delete his (or her) profile from online dating sites, that would be a good thing. And if serial killers and total psychos were to follow suit, that would be even better. Then all we'd have to worry about is everybody else, those supposedly normal people who for whatever reason—fear, indecision, even kindness—might not be completely up-front with us about how they really feel, who might say things that aren't true, who might lead us on or push us away when they really want to let us go or pull us in.

Knowing when you can trust in love is hard. Sometimes it feels impossible. You have to figure out by yourself whom to trust and why, following your own instincts, and without being too naïve or too paranoid. A used-car dealer may respect you for giving him a hard time and acting suspicious of his claims. But during the fragile uncertainty of a relationship's early days, acting suspicious could spell doom.

Given how difficult everyone knows the task can be and how susceptible we all are to the allure of some sexy stranger flirting with us, why are we so eager to ridicule those who have trusted unwisely? We roundly condemn those who fall for cons or liars as total fools. Yet are we really so sure we would know better?

Let's have a look at how three cases that captured attention in recent years played out in the court of public opinion.

Case 1: The Foolish Jock

Manti Te'o, a star Notre Dame football player who supposedly fell for a woman he met online in 2011, was widely mocked as a thick-necked cretin for having publicly proclaimed his love for someone who turned out not to exist. To friends, family, and the media, he talked about Lennay Kekua as his girlfriend, the love of his life, and even his future wife. When she abruptly died of leukemia near the start of Notre Dame's 2012 football season (only two weeks after her surprise diagnosis, and on the same day Te'o's grandmother died), Manti Te'o's tragic love story went national, and his spirited play in the first games of Notre Dame's season was credited to his emotional outpouring in the midst of so much personal tragedy.

When it came to light many months later that Lennay Kekua never existed, and Te'o had never met her, and neither had his family, the public was incredulous. Her picture was of someone else, swiped off the Internet, and her voice—those few times they spoke on the phone—was, oddly enough, that of a male football player who had briefly crossed paths with Te'o years before and who went on to describe himself in media interviews as a "recovering homosexual."

The reaction in the press was basically: Who could be so stupid? Some argued Te'o had to be complicit in the hoax, perhaps to deflect rumors of his own homosexuality, because no other explanation could be credible. When Te'o embarked on a series of media appearances, though, and didn't exactly come across as the sharpest tool in the shed, his gullibility seemed easier to believe than his culpability.

In any event, the court of public opinion already had made up its mind.

The verdict? Fool.

Case 2: The Foolish Ivy League Grad

Sandra Boss received similar treatment from the public and the press, even though she was seduced and conned in person. She actually married someone who didn't exist, lived with him for twelve years, and gave birth to his daughter. The man she fell for called himself Clark Rockefeller. But there was no such person, no tie to the famous Rockefeller family (as he'd claimed), no art collection that constituted his imaginary wealth, no New England childhood of summer camps and sailing. Clark Rockefeller was the creation of Christian Karl Gerhartsreiter, a German immigrant with a checkered past and serious mental health issues.

While in graduate school in Cambridge, Sandra believed this man's false identity and fell in love with him. No intellectual slouch, she had gone to Stanford and then to Harvard Business School. As a young professional woman, early in their marriage, she was already earning in excess of a million dollars a year. She seemed intelligent, poised, articulate, attractive, and successful in every imaginable way. Yet she had built her life around a husband whose identity was an utter fabrication, a man with no driver's license, medical records, income, or evidence of his supposed vast wealth. Ultimately the authorities would learn that he had married a woman in Wisconsin and murdered a man in San Diego (and perhaps the man's wife, too), so Boss was far from the only person he had fooled. He even managed to charm his way onto the board of directors of the exclusive Algonquin Club.

His scheme unraveled when Boss, long suspicious and finally having mustered the wherewithal to do something about it, hired a private investigator who promptly began to pull back the curtain on Christian Gerhartsreiter's grand-scale deceit. With the truth emerging, Boss sought a divorce and custody of their daughter. But after she was awarded custody, her ex kidnapped the girl and fled. Eventually he was caught in a condominium he'd purchased with Boss's money in Baltimore.

During her ex-husband's trial on kidnapping charges, Boss was pressed on the witness stand to explain how she, as an ostensibly educated person, possibly could have fallen for this man's lies.

"There's a big difference between intellectual intelligence and emotional intelligence," she explained. "I'm not saying I made a very good choice in a husband. It's obvious I have a pretty big blind spot. All I'm saying is that it's possible that one can be brilliant and amazing in one area of one's life yet pretty stupid in another."

The media savaged her, calling her a "dingbat doormat" who had fallen for a "Crockafeller."

The court of public opinion agreed. Its verdict? Fool.

Case 3: The Foolish Professor of Particle Physics

Paul Frampton, a sixty-eight-year-old particle physicist and Nobel Prize contender from North Carolina whose story was chronicled in the *New York Times Magazine* in May of 2013 was divorced and lonely. He wanted love, children, and a fresh start. So he began looking online. Soon he met a woman on the dating site Mate1.com. She claimed to be the famous Czech bikini model Denise Milani, who was thirty-seven years younger than him and had triple-D-size breasts. If you type her name into Google, you'll be able to see a zillion pictures of those triple-Ds yourself.

Lo and behold, she was really interested in him. What luck!

Since Frampton wanted children, it made the most sense for him to pair up with someone young and beautiful who would be fertile and produce gorgeous offspring. Big breasts are a sign of fertility, right? And the fact that Denise Milani was coming on to him was icing on the cake. She told him she really wanted children too and was sick of all this international modeling crap. What she really wanted was to settle down with an aging professor like him and have a happy family. He had brains. She had a body. It was a perfect combination.

So he headed off to meet her in Bolivia, where she was on a photo shoot. But when he arrived, it turned out she had been called away for a modeling gig in Brussels. Damn. She wanted to know if he could perhaps get on a plane and join her there. Sure he could.

Oh, and if he could just pick up a suitcase she'd left behind in La Paz and bring it along to Brussels, she'd be ever so grateful.

When a pal of Frampton's in Canada got wind of this improbable globe-trotting love affair, he was alarmed and warned his friend to stop all contact with the woman immediately. The person who was writing to him couldn't be that famous Czech model, the friend argued. What in the world was Frampton thinking? And definitely, the friend urged, do *not*, under any circumstances, take that suitcase on board any flight. It will be full of drugs, he bluntly predicted.

The professor cheerfully ignored his friend's advice. He was in love with Denise Milani, and she was in love with him, and that's all there was to it.

When it was discovered (during his connection in Buenos Aires) that the suitcase was indeed loaded with cocaine, Frampton was promptly arrested and thrown in jail. Later a reporter asked him why he hadn't heeded his colleague's admonition that a world-famous Czech bikini model would never pursue someone like him, and that it couldn't be her flirting with him online but was probably a criminal. What made him ignore his friend and believe in it anyway?

"I have been accused of having a huge ego," the professor answered.

In an Argentinean court, that ego earned Frampton a sentence of eight years and four months in prison for drug trafficking. Separately, the court of public opinion handed down its own opinion. The verdict? Fool.

SO THERE YOU HAVE IT: ONLY fools fall for liars. We have nothing to worry about as long as we're not complete idiots, right?

I wish I could join in the blanket condemnation of Manti Te'o, Sandra Boss, and Paul Frampton, but I've seen too many people fall for too many lies to be so sure that a lot of us wouldn't do the same thing under similar circumstances. Whether we choose to believe the lies of a con artist, the alibis of a philandering spouse, or the feigned affection of someone who simply doesn't have the courage to admit that he or she doesn't really love us, our fundamental gullibility is the same. We like to believe in love, and love requires a certain amount of trust. Plus, it's nicer to think attractive people are attracted to us than to suspect we're not worthy of such attention. The nature and motivation of the lying may be different, but in each case our desire to believe in love is stronger than our instinct to doubt it.

We imagine that signs of deceit or false flattery should be obvious, and that we ought to be smart enough to know the difference. But most of the people I've heard from who fell for the most outrageous of cons were all articulate, highly educated, and well-compensated professionals just like Sandra Boss and Paul Frampton, whether they were executives in the financial services industry or college professors at elite universities. Evidently these people were not fools at work or fools in life. They had not been fools in childhood or fools in school. They were only, as is so often the case, fools in love.

So how can we trust in love while making sure we can't be hurt, lied to, or taken advantage of? Nobody really knows—certainly not the scolds and the ridiculers. And neither, apparently, do the self-proclaimed experts. From the help sections of online dating sites to the hosts of daytime television, glib advice is plentiful and perhaps well-intentioned but usually is worth about as much as it costs: nothing. If you want to hear what they have to say anyway, I've provided boiled-down versions of a few common tips below (just please don't follow them).

Avoid Everybody

The warning signs for cons on online dating sites are a prime example of how impossible it is to steer people clear of danger. Most services provide tips on what to look out for, but they're almost comically unhelpful.

"Con men look more average than ever," yawns the first tip on eHarmony.

"Con men are more subtle than ever," suggests the next.

The third? "Con men are no longer in a hurry."

So there you have it. If some average-looking guy subtly comes on to you without exerting any pressure, call the FBI immediately.

Wait, there's more. The con man will act curious about who you are and where you're from and what you like, not because he's interested in you as a person but because he's searching for anything that might be used to answer your online banking security questions. I suppose that means if the person you're falling in love with asks where you grew up, you might want to be vague or say you used to know but forgot. And if he asks if you had any childhood pets, say you did but explain that in your family, pets had no names. Your first teacher didn't have a name either, at least none you can recall. And no, you don't have a favorite movie star ("They're all so good!").

If the guy you're interested in seems especially decent, a generous provider who has various people (children, parents, extended family) who depend on him for care, comfort, food, or love, that's a huge red flag; he may use that supposed dependency as a ruse to guilt you into wiring him money. If he himself is in need of medical care (or seems like he will be at some point), that also should set off major alarm bells, because if you love him and he claims to need treatment he can't otherwise afford, you might be willing to kick in for it, and then there goes your bank account, straight to Nigeria.

So just to be safe, it's probably best to avoid anyone who seems poor and might have an excuse to ask for money. It's also a good idea to avoid anyone who acts like he's rich, because that may just be a trick to make him seem impressive and alluring. Keep in mind, though, that today's con artists strive to be average in every way, so it's wise to steer clear of anyone who acts like he's middle-class as well.

The most sophisticated con artists will have created a credible presence on LinkedIn, Twitter, Facebook, and wherever else you might look to verify their identity and learn more about them. They'll probably have posted family photos and accumulated a tweeting history and a have respectable number of followers and friends. In short, they will seem like normal people leading normal lives who have hopes and dreams just like everyone else. So be extra-vigilant if you ever meet someone like that.

Last but not least, eHarmony suggests you be wary if anyone you don't know and haven't met asks outright for your money, your banking information, and/or access to your online financial accounts.

Um, yeah.

Conduct Extensive Online Background Checks

When dating so many strangers, we naturally try to find out as much about people as we can as soon as possible. Technology may give us a screen to hide behind, but at the same time it provides us with the tools to become armchair detectives and conduct our own extensive background checks. With the help of Google, Facebook, Instagram, Twitter, LinkedIn, and many other social media and search sites, we can be scrolling through potential lovers' life histories, friendships, previous relationships, careers, writing samples, and achievements before we've met, spoken, or even corresponded.

When investigating future dates, we often think the more we can learn the better. But learning too much too soon from this glut of information can have surprising downsides. Take the example of Joanna, who soon after college got a job as a program officer at an AIDS nonprofit in Washington, DC. One night while out with friends, she met a guy in a Georgetown bar who was unusually tall (as she was) and ran (like she did) and charmed her from the start. When he mentioned that he liked to run, she joked that if they ever went running together she'd "leave him in the dust."

A few days later he called and asked her out. That's when she decided, as anyone would, to Google him. And she was able to quickly confirm that he did indeed like to run. He ran well. Really well! In fact, he was an Olympic-caliber miler who'd broken the famous four-minute mark. And that wasn't all. She had just scratched the surface of his information iceberg. During the next several hours she would find out much more, poring over whatever she could find on his educational background (his Ivy League GPA, his MBA program), writings (published essays and articles), family (including info on his siblings), business philosophies, trips he'd taken, favorite hamburger joint, the neighborhood he grew up in . . . and on and on.

The day of their date, Joanna got her first facial, which unfortunately left her with raw cheeks and a chin abrasion, adding to her insecurity. But it wasn't until they got to the bar and starting drinking wine that the trouble really began. She had so much information about him in her head that the typical small talk one might have early in a date was rendered meaningless. But she couldn't admit to everything she knew about him. It might be honest to say she'd Googled him and discovered a few things, but she was way beyond knowing just a few things.

At first she tried to tease out his background anyway, just so a lot of what she'd learned would become fair game for conversation. But as he told her details of his life she already knew, she worried that her reactions weren't authentic, or were delayed.

When he told her he'd run a sub-four-minute mile, for instance, she didn't react at all at first and instead thought, *Yeah, by one second.* Then she realized her mistake and acted surprised by his remarkable feat way too late.

The longer it went and the more she drank, the more flustered she became. At one point he told some story about his brother, which prompted Joanna to say, "So it's you, your brother, and your sister?"

"Did I tell you about her?" he asked.

Had he? "No, no," she sputtered. "Do you have a sister?"

It was hopeless; she simply knew too much and had drunk too much and could no longer tell the difference. And she was in too deep by then to suddenly come clean about having learned everything about him beforehand.

Later that evening the date ended unremarkably and unromantically, and they never went out again. The lesson Joanna learned? As she put it: "There's something to be said for the spontaneity and authentic facial expressions of utter ignorance."

Be Realistic About Who Might Love You

Dr. Phil has advice about love scams, in case you were wondering. How could he not? Love scams are tailor-made for daytime talk shows, full of heartbreak and ridicule and audience incredulity. You just need to plop a few victims onstage, let them tell their sorry tales of losing their savings, allow the audience to gasp and point as if they're gawking at apes in the zoo, and then, when it's all over, close out the segment with a sigh of seeming concern and deliver your parting shot of wisdom: "If something sounds too good to be true, it probably is."

Come on, Phil. Can't you do better than that? You're a doctor, after all (I think). We really could use your psychological expertise on this one. The old "sounds too good to be true" bromide might be good advice if you're warning someone against paying a suspiciously low price for some luxury product. But when it comes to love, isn't "too good to be true" exactly what a lot of us are looking for?

If we're not feeling giddy with disbelief about our inexplicable good fortune in having met this person, we're probably going to question whether this relationship is even worth pursuing. Far from being love's red flag, "too good to be true," for many, is love's baseline expectation.

In Dr. Phil's defense, that same pearl of wisdom appears on love-scam warning lists from one end of the Internet to the other. We are told repeatedly that if someone who seems out of our league or is "too perfect" acts interested in us, we might want to be tight-lipped about our birthplace, favorite gemstone, and the name of the street we lived on in third grade. And as one source suggests, we might want to proceed with caution (or full-blown paranoia) by asking them to send us a picture of themselves holding a current issue of their local paper, with the date visible and their screen name scrawled across the top, just to, you know, prove to us that they're real—or for us to prove to them that we're nuts, whatever the case may be.

Anyway, there's no generally accepted standard for "too good to be true" in matters of the heart. For people with low self-esteem, any attention might seem too good to be true, whereas for someone with a healthy ego like our friend Paul Frampton, being pursued by an internationally famous supermodel may seem completely reasonable.

The real question is this: If "too good to be true" is to serve as our litmus test, and we end up backing away from someone for that reason, how are we supposed to know if we're saving ourselves from being conned by the wrong person or conning ourselves out of being loved by the right one?

WHY DO FOOLS FALL IN LOVE?

I TEND TO be more trusting and optimistic than Cathi (the two characteristics often go hand in hand). For example, she typically will greet good news with skepticism, anticipating the explanation of how the good news isn't really so good after all, while I am more likely to embrace the good news and then be disappointed when it turns out to less wonderful than it first seemed.

During our months of writing letters we were establishing trust, or so I thought. But we'd only met in person for an hour or so during our Tucson lunch, and we hadn't spoken on the phone at all, so we really didn't have much to go on. I knew only what she told me about herself in letters, and she knew only what I told her, and both of us were trying to make ourselves look good, which may not have involved outright lying but also didn't necessarily lead to complete truth telling.

Eventually an opportunity arose for us to spend a long weekend together when a friend of hers in San Antonio—an ex-boyfriend, actually—contacted her about doing an apartment swap: he was traveling to New York for three days and wanted to know if she had any interest in going to San Antonio.

So she floated the idea to me. I was immediately on board. Like I said, I embrace good news. Then came the inevitable downer: she wrote back shortly before the trip to say maybe it would be best if our relationship remained platonic for the weekend, with me on the couch and her in the bedroom, as friends just getting to know each other. The obvious subtext being: she didn't trust me yet, or didn't fully trust the situation, and she wanted to protect herself.

I agreed to her terms (what choice did I have?), though I admit that given the ground rules I wasn't looking forward to the trip as much as I once had been, and I even wondered if she was getting cold feet and this was the beginning of her exit strategy. I went anyway with high hopes, and at the start everything went as planned. Our relationship remained platonic for the first several hours, from when she picked me up at the airport, through our dinner out, and back at the condo, where we sat on the couch together, keeping our hands to ourselves and talking. Always a rule follower, I was grimly prepared to go the distance, but apparently Cathi wasn't, and soon the wall she'd put up between us came tumbling down.

The next morning, when I asked why she ever expected us to keep our physical distance for the whole visit, she said, "I was just being cautious. After all, I don't even really know you."

And I thought: *You don't even know me? What do you mean you don't even know me? I'm me!*

Well, yeah. I was me to me, but I wasn't yet me to her, if that makes any sense. Meaning: I knew myself, believed that I was honest and kind and trustworthy, and I was surprised to think that anyone who'd gotten to know me at all could possibly be wary of me. Then again, it's easier to trust blindly when—as in my case—you're stronger, taller, and outweigh the other person by double. Even so, I trusted her implicitly, and she didn't trust me, at least not at first. Yet she was also more generally skeptical of love than I was. I had a healthy enough ego to believe she would want to have a relationship with me. As with most relationships I entered into, I didn't go in worrying I'd be lied to or victimized or even hurt.

Who knows, if some husky-voiced woman calling herself Lennay Kekua were to reach out to me online and flirt with me for months via messaging and phone calls, would I believe that she was a real person and take the bait? Or would I suspect she was really a male ex–football player I once knew who had developed a same-sex crush on me and whose intentions were questionable?

For a lot of reasons, I think I'd believe she was a real person who was honestly flirting with me.

So what about the Sandra Boss scenario? Would I allow myself to fall in love with and eventually marry some woman I'd met in Cambridge while attending Harvard Business School? If she claimed she was a Rockefeller, would I believe her without asking for medical records, tax statements, or other documentation? And might I fall in love with her?

If she was convincing enough (as sociopaths typically are), I probably would. After all, it would be cool to tell everyone I was dating a Rockefeller, especially one who claimed to love me so much.

And what about the third scenario? Might I believe that an

internationally famous Czech bikini model would seek me out online and want to retire from modeling at the peak of her career so she could start a family with me in North Carolina?

No, I have to say I wouldn't believe that one. My ego is healthy but not that healthy. Not that I don't give Paul Frampton credit for being so open to the possibilities of love that he did believe it. After all, love is for people who are ready to dream big and risk everything.

Unfortunately, so is prison.

6

Practicality

LOVE'S FLUORESCENTLY LIT CLASSROOM

CATHI AND I GOT ENGAGED ON a ferryboat in San Francisco Bay. Romantic, right? Not for us. We had departed from Fisherman's Wharf, bound for Sausalito, when Cathi said, "So, are we getting married, or what?"

"Yeah, we should," I said.

And that was it. We had become engaged. Even though I hadn't proposed. Hadn't knelt. Hadn't pulled a hidden ring box from my pocket or sock and presented it to her with a big, goofy smile. Hadn't memorized or delivered any heartfelt lines. I don't even think we kissed.

By then we had been together for almost two years. We were both twenty-nine years old, nearing the end of our graduate school days (I was already finished), and obviously had to figure out what was next for us. Our marriage and family clock was ticking, and our parents' expectations were mounting. I wanted to marry Cathi and assumed we would get married, and yet I hadn't taken a single step in that direction.

Why hadn't I? I wish I could claim some standard excuse like commitment issues or a laundry list of doubts, but it wouldn't be true. I wasn't worried about Cathi specifically or about marriage generally. I expected it would all work out fine. I wasn't concerned about joining her family or her joining mine. I was simply procrastinating because I didn't want to face the work and stress that proposing and then planning a wedding would require.

As we steamed past Alcatraz Island (no prison symbolism intended), Cathi asked if I had any thoughts about a ring.

"No," I said. "But I'll ask my mother."

Oof.

It's nice to think that love is all about sex and fun times and floating along on a river of bliss, but sooner or later we have to face the work of love. Planning a wedding is a perfect example. I keep hearing from newly engaged couples, disillusioned by the commercial and practical demands of wedding planning, who erupt in rants like, "Why does getting married have to be such a huge nightmare? This is supposed to be about love! All this stress just makes us want to skip the whole thing and elope."

Which is sort of like an aspiring marine asking, "Why do they have to make boot camp so hard? What's the deal with all of the push-ups and inspections and yelling? That's just going to turn people off from wanting to be marines."

If you can't survive boot camp, chances are you won't survive being a marine. Likewise, if you can't navigate the stresses and complexities of wedding planning, you probably aren't going to get very far in marriage. Planning a wedding is like boot camp for planning a life; you get to sample the various ways marriage will test you. You have to work with your future spouse to address the same kinds of questions you'll be grappling with as a couple for the rest of your lives: What will we eat? What will we say? What will people think of us? What kind of appliances and bath towels do we need/like? How can we pay for this? How will we manage the needs and egos of our friends and family? Once you commit and head down this road, you will inevitably start spending less time in the "tiki bar" phase of your relationship (with the fruity drinks and line dancing and sexy sarongs) and more in the "fluorescently lit classroom" phase of hard desks, steel chairs, and number 2 pencils.

That classroom, sorry to say, is where this chapter takes place. The material we'll cover may not sound like much fun, and I can assure you it's not. But if you don't invest a good chunk of time in a few fluorescently lit classrooms early in your relationship, dutifully discussing the terms of your marriage and family life, you may end up spending that time in a fluorescently lit lawyer's office instead, glumly negotiating the terms of your divorce.

Ready? Our Marriage 101 syllabus begins with "Individuality" (as in, losing it), segues into "Identity" (in terms of choosing a last name for your new family), and wraps up with "Equality" (of income, child care, and chores).

Except for choosing your family name, which typically requires a decision by your wedding day, these issues may trouble you for a lifetime, or at least for the length of your marriage (whichever ends first). So if you can't figure out how best to handle a certain situation, relax: you probably never will. My wife and I have been no more successful at solving these issues than anyone, but at least I can try to provide you with some of the highlights and lowlights of what others have tried. Maybe hearing about their attempts will help you do better.

1. MAINTAINING INDIVIDUALITY IN MARRIAGE

I HEAR FREQUENTLY from twenty- and thirtysomethings who worry about losing their individuality when they get married. For many, it's their greatest fear. In exploring the roots of their anxiety, they sift through painful memories of their parents' marriage, wishing there had been more sweetness and less arguing. Often the portrait they paint is one of sublimated desires, of personal dreams sacrificed on the altar of marriage and parenthood. These young newlyweds and not-yet-weds vow they're not going to let the same thing happen to them. They're going to do marriage better by fighting to preserve their essential individuality in a way their parents weren't able to due to societal pressures or entrenched roles or whatever.

Yet even the most idealistic among them generally concede that getting married does, in fact, mean the end of being single. They grudgingly accept the game-show rule that says when you choose the new living room ensemble behind door number 2 you don't also get to keep the fabulous Jet Ski package that was behind door number one.

Still, we wish there were a better way to combine the benefits of marriage and family life (stability, tax breaks, commitment, social acceptability, someone to care for us when we're sick or old) with the premium aspects of remaining single (solitude, sexual freedom, flexibility, spontaneity). Even as marriages become more egalitarian and accommodating to individual needs in many ways, we're constantly fiddling with the dial, searching for a more static-free mix of commitment and freedom.

If losing your individuality in marriage concerns you, here are some ways you might try to keep your private pilot light from being snuffed out. Some may seem a little unusual, inviting criticism from family and friends. But as with anything, the more people do them the less unusual they'll seem.

Keeping Separate Houses

Being stuck in the same house with the same person for life can be a problem for married people. For some, it's smothering. All that marital and family togetherness feels wonderful to a point, but there's a fine line between coziness and claustrophobia. As a solution, more than a few women I've heard from over the years (my wife among them) have floated the idea of having separate houses for husbands and wives.

Um, isn't that divorce? Not in this case. These wives don't want a divorce. They love their husbands (or so they claim) along with a lot of the other benefits of marriage and family life. They just wish they could have more physical space built into the marriage, perhaps in the form of a little house right next door to their husband's house where they could live part-time. Not a big house, necessarily; just a cabin or studio apartment or even a nice, heated, renovated storage shed in the backyard. In this house would be their cherished personal items: a little refrigerator that wouldn't always be raided by everyone, a window seat for reading and drinking tea, a yoga mat for exercise and meditation, and a single bed for sleeping. They could sleep in their single bed sometimes and sleep in the house with their husband sometimes. But doing so would be a choice, not an obligation. And that would make all the difference.

Cathi and I actually tried this during the first six months of our marriage, though for us it was more about practicality than idealism. We married at the end of June, and we knew we'd be moving from Tucson to New York in January, so it made little sense for us to give up our separate, small, cheap places and rent a joint house or apartment for only half a year.

And as two creative people who value solitude, we liked it (Cathi more than I, admittedly). Sometimes we slept at her house, sometimes we slept at mine, and sometimes we stayed at our own places. It was only awkward when I had to talk about "my wife's house" while trying to explain that we weren't divorced or separated, which was way more than anyone (like the cable repair guy) needed or wanted to know.

Of course, adding children and pets and busy lives to the equation complicates things. And buying and maintaining separate residences, even if it's just a renovated Tuff Shed next to the garage, can be costly (though surely cheaper than divorce). But that doesn't stop many, including my dear wife, from yearning for it. Every so often Cathi will still say to me wistfully, "Remember when we each had our own house in Tucson? That was total heaven."

Total heaven, in our case, that relied on us being married and committed but with the flexibility to live apart.

Acting a Little Divorced

In a similar vein, some hope to maintain their individuality in marriage by acting a little divorced. Not by getting divorced, but by trying to incorporate the benefits of divorce into their marriage.

Rachel and her husband had both been children of divorce, and they were determined to make their own marriage last. Yet Rachel chafed against many of marriage's downsides. Although she and her husband had worked hard to be caring and committed partners (in trying to avoid their parents' fate), they still had defaulted to mostly traditional roles as husband and wife, a failing Rachel blamed on the malaise that often accompanies giving up one's independence.

She did more with the children, including the cooking and shopping, even though her husband had had all those skills when he was single and, once married, had simply let them wither. She used to be bolder as a single woman about pursuing things she wanted to do, yet in marriage she had begun to feel meeker and more sheltered—and much more prone to guilt. Recently she even had talked herself out of accepting an opportunity to go to Paris by surrendering to worries about leaving her children and fearing she'd be too distracted by having abandoned her family to enjoy herself anyway. She also lamented that marriage had allowed her husband to let go of his male friendships, making him more reliant on her and the children for his social life, a typical pattern for many married men.

As the first wave of Rachel's contemporaries with young children began to divorce, she wasn't surprised to feel sad for them and the emotional turmoil they had to endure. She was surprised, however, to feel envy. Not for the heartache or financial drain or acrimony, none of which she would welcome into her own life. Nor for the stark separation from the man she loved. But she was struck by how often she heard people say things like, "He's such a great dad ever since the divorce," along with stories of women pursuing long-thwarted dreams and rediscovering themselves in deeply satisfying ways postdivorce.

Their divorced friends, she observed, had become admirably self-sufficient in ways she and her husband weren't. They had reclaimed some of what they'd lost to marriage. Out of necessity, the fathers had to step in and do everything when the kids were with them, so they regained their shopping and cooking skills, at least somewhat. They also had to oversee homework on their own and deal with school administrators and teachers and soccer coaches and doctors.

And they had to take care of themselves, too, breaking out of the lazy, family-centric social patterns that had left them insular and unsocial. The women also had regained skills that had withered in marriage—from fixing toilets to paying bills to putting air in the car tires—along with active social lives when they weren't the custodial parent.

Rachel knew that many fathers don't rise to these challenges postmarriage, and that some remarry quickly and expect their new wife to take care of them and fill the voids in their social lives the same way the old wife did. She didn't want to glorify divorce or get divorced herself. But might it be possible, she wondered, to cherry-pick some of the benefits? Could they act a little divorced without actually having to get divorced?

It seemed the answer should be yes, but doing so would require a trick of the mind and a willful change in habits. The trick would be to remind yourself, constantly, that you ought to be as able and independent within marriage as without it. The change in habits would require you to leave your spouse in charge of the house and children as if you were handing off those responsibilities to him or her as part of your custody arrangement. In your time as the noncustodial parent, you'd have to make yourself get out and do whatever you would if you were legally barred from taking responsibility during those times.

And that means, at the least, you should be able to take that trip to Paris (or even just to Poughkeepsie) and not feel guilty about it.

Having an Open Marriage

For some the biggest drawback of marriage is committing to having sex with the same person for the rest of their lives, and they'd like to be able to "opt out" of that particular restriction. Some actually do opt out by agreeing to have an open marriage.

In such an arrangement, also known as polyamory—or just "poly" for those who can't be troubled with adding the "amory"—you are allowed to have sex with other people, and so is your spouse. This can be a proposition fraught with peril even for the most free-spirited and open-minded couples, so typically the first thing they'll do is come up with a set of rules and expectations to govern their behavior. Some even write these rules down (but probably don't post them on their refrigerator).

Rules might include: No lying, no overnights, must use protection, no falling in love, never bring your lover back to the house.

Such lists can go on and on, trying to provide for every eventuality.

One couple I heard from acknowledged that they'd needed rules before embarking on an open arrangement, but they felt presumptuous trying to come up with guidelines for affairs they assumed would happen but perhaps wouldn't. Relationships are unpredictable even under normal circumstances. Were they really going to slave over a rule book that assumed anybody even would want to have sex with them when they were already married? And not just anybody, but someone they actually wanted to have sex with? The complexities raised by their discussion alone already had them a little freaked out.

They had started down the open-marriage road for the same reason couples often do—because one of them (in this case, the husband) wanted to be able to explore his feelings for a female friend who'd admitted she had a crush on him. The wife happened to know the woman and liked and respected her, so she did have a certain comfort level with their mutual affection. Also, the wife had been in open relationships before she met her husband, and she wanted to be flexible and freethinking within marriage as long as it didn't threaten what they had (a big if). Plus, she worried that if she were to clamp down their marriage and forbid her husband from seeing the woman or anyone else, it only would lead to sublimated desires, fantasizing, lying, and cheating. If you love someone, set him free, right?

In their case there was yet another wrinkle. She had developed a crush on someone, too, a work colleague, and now that her husband had raised the issue and she'd agreed to it in theory, she wondered about exploring that interest (sex with the colleague) with her hubby's permission. Aside from her standard worries about jealousy, though, she had logistical concerns. For example, should she try to plan her time with her colleague to coincide with her husband's night out with his friend? Did she and her husband need to tell each other whenever they wanted to go out with their extramarital would-be lovers? What were the rules?

They agreed their most important spoken rule would be "No lying." But the most important unspoken rule with such couples tends to be "No jealousy," because that often proves to be the greatest challenge. As always, rules governing emotions seem to make more sense in theory than in practice. You can tell yourself that jealousy is "just a feeling" that shouldn't apply since you love each other and are allowing the behavior, and you need to rise above it. You can try to convince yourself that truly loving someone means not denying him or her pleasure. You can ask God to grant you the serenity to accept the things you cannot change, the courage to change the things you can, and the wisdom to know the difference.

Yet in the end you still might wind up totally losing your shit when your spouse is off having sex with someone else, with your permission, while you're stuck at home alone watching *The Bachelor*.

Even the most delicately handled open-marriage arrangements can be riddled with emotional land mines that can be tripped with the slightest stumble or wayward step. With this particular couple, two developments led to the unraveling of their arrangement.

The wife's dalliance ended first. The work colleague she had been flirting with was intrigued by the possibility but ultimately couldn't deal with the reality of participating in an open marriage as the "other guy." He was uneasy about the moral implications, yes, but his reluctance was also quite simple: He didn't want to get hurt. He didn't want to risk falling in love with someone who wasn't available. And from what I've seen, his hesitation was well founded. Often the real victim in an open marriage is not the couple, who have each other to fall back on, but the outsider, who gets left out.

Meanwhile, the husband and his friend were having a lot of presumably innocent fun together, taking pictures and spending time developing them (hmmm . . . in a darkroom?). They hadn't gotten physical yet. But one night he called his wife to say he'd be home late because their car wouldn't start, and she wondered if he was telling the truth. It was an old Volvo that she knew was unreliable, so she shouldn't doubt him, but she did doubt him, so the result was the same. As she discovered, feeling doubt can have the same destructive effect as actually being lied to, whether or not that doubt is warranted. It eats away at your sense of trust regardless.

After several arguments and ten therapy sessions, this couple was able to put their romantic safari in the rearview mirror, grateful they hadn't taken the experiment any further. In open marriages that do take hold, the partners may engage in the same kind of skirmishes over fairness and equality that infuse all aspects of contemporary marriage, a feeling that each should be taking advantage of their sexual freedom in roughly equal amounts (number of partners) and to equal degrees (how much and what kind of sexual contact). If the wife is going out with several people and the husband is only seeing one, it might start to have an impact on the arrangement even if the husband doesn't want more, just because it feels unfair. I've actually heard from people in open marriages mulling how many flings they were "entitled" to, based on their spouse's track record so far—a level of bean-counting and pettiness that seems contrary to the whole notion of personal and sexual freedom and creativity that open marriage is supposed to be about.

The final reckoning for couples who do succeed in having an open arrangement, at least for a while, often comes with the arrival of children. Babies have a way of changing the family dynamic regardless, making the marriage less about sex and self-fulfillment and more about nesting and security. Perhaps this shift also redirects the couple's gaze from their own needs to someone else's. And as the kiddos get older and more aware of what's going on around them (such as to things that go hump in the night), practical hurdles can arise, like keeping them from finding out, which may involve the very kind of deception you were trying to avoid in being "open."

At least until the day you sit down with your glum teens for a frank discussion about having safe and responsible sex. That's when you can explain that this is something you are still dealing with, too, because mommy and daddy sometimes sleep around with other people's mommies and daddies and so are also concerned about STDs and unplanned pregnancies. Just like you and your friends!

Acquiring an Office Spouse

This is a popular option for working couples who aren't getting all they need from their primary relationship and want extra attention and adoration without the risks of sex.

In the old days of stark inequality in the office, men often sexually preyed on the women who worked for them. Now, while sexual preying still exists, the vibe is more balanced, and platonic office-spouse relationships—where neither partner is intimidator or intimidatee—are flourishing. In fact, they are filling a desperate need, because in many marriages today no one takes care of the poor full-time worker when he or she comes home exhausted from another grueling day at the office.

Who can be available for that when both spouses come home exhausted from another grueling day at the office? Not only do they walk in the door at seven or eight P.M. without the expectation of a smile, a dinner, a drink, or a back massage, they also know they face their exhausting second shift of home and child-care responsibilities. The last thing they have the energy for is listening to or comforting their partner. So these attention-deprived spouses are seeking that comfort at the office, which is where they're spending the vast majority of their waking hours anyway.

An office spouse is someone you like and maybe flirt with but don't have sex with. This means you have to be careful not to cross certain boundaries or it can get really messy—even messier than an open marriage.

Some acceptable subjects to talk about with your office spouse? Work, news and current events, hobbies, your children, and family vacations. Preapproved activities might include texting or calling at home about work, going out to lunch, exchanging birthday gifts, and watching funny YouTube videos together in the office.

Some topics to avoid discussing with your office spouse might be marital troubles, divorce fantasies, and sexual fantasies. Discouraged activities include telling dirty jokes, exchanging Valentine's gifts, and watching online porn in the office (or out).

You also might want to refrain from asking speculative questions of your office spouse, such as, "I wonder if we would have made a good couple?" or "What do you think it would be like if we were to kiss?"

One depressing note about office-spouse relationships in today's economy, with so many people losing their jobs, is that with office layoffs come office divorces. But unlike in a real marriage, where there's both a process for the breakup and a reason that it's happening, there's typically neither cause nor method for an office divorce. You are forced to break up cold turkey from someone you may feel as close to as your actual spouse—or closer, in some cases—often with little warning. And it can be difficult to keep up the relationship afterward, no matter how much it meant to you. In the end, your only continued tie to the person in whom you'd invested more emotional energy over the years than anyone else may be the folder of his or her unfinished work that gets dumped on your desk.

2. CREATING FAIRER FAMILY NAMES

THE SECOND SUBJECT in my premarriage syllabus involves figuring out a last name for your new family. These days many people want something that's inclusive, unifying, and nonpatriarchal, while also not saddling their children with some multihyphenated, multisurnamed monstrosity. (Smith-Sullivan-Schwartzfelder-Abramowitz, anyone?)

In nine years of seeing people struggle with this issue, I have yet to come across anyone who has answered it satisfactorily—no one, at any rate, who has been able to meet the above-stated requirements of a better family name. First, coming up with a name that doesn't somehow honor the patriarchy appears to be impossible, since, frankly, everything honors the patriarchy: combined names, women's last names (which tend to come from their fathers), or pieces of names (which come from both fathers).

Unless you make up a name that's pure nonsense, like when Prince changed his name to that bizarre symbol, forcing everyone to refer to him as "The Artist Formerly Known as Prince," you're always going to be honoring the patriarchy. Even Prince's unspeakable symbol surely had its roots in the patriarchy, resembling, as it did, some twisted combination of a dagger and a phallus. And this isn't just a male/female issue either, plaguing only heterosexual relationships. Gay fathers are stuck with the patriarchy for obvious reasons when it comes to names, and so are lesbian mothers, ironically enough. So maybe we should just set that one aside until we acquire a higher level of brainpower capable of addressing it.

That doesn't mean in the interim we won't continue to have naming needs and shouldn't keep trying new formulations. And the good news is we seem to be in the midst of a creative-naming boomlet, with all kinds of fun and experimental options being floated and halfheartedly embraced. Here's a rundown of available choices, with pros and cons for each. Alas, none are without cons.

Full Patriarchy
(Wife and kids both take husband's surname—same as it ever was.)

Pros: Everyone has the same surname, clearing the way for easier identification with travel, work, schools, etc. Also, if the wife was saddled with an embarrassing maiden name that has long subjected her to teasing, like "Bottcrack," or a silly-sounding first/last combo, like "Sandy Bottcrack," then taking her husband's name might provide a chance at a fresh start ("Sandy Wilson").

Cons: Possible loss of female identity. Childhood friends can't find you without your maiden name. You have to use the term "maiden name," which might make you feel like a throwback to a previous century. Potential for male guilt and shame over continuing unjust patriarchal practice. Teaches your kids that status quo is acceptable, thus propagating the injustice. Raises thorny issue of husband attempting to "possess" wife by stamping his name on her. Can be seen by some as wimpy, retro. Women might look down at other women for surrendering to it, causing rifts.

Partial Patriarchy
(Wife keeps her surname but kids take husband's surname.)

Pros: Name unity with husband and kids. Wife's identity remains strong. A lot of people do it this way, so perhaps there will be less judgment.

Cons: Wife may feel estranged from rest of family. Creates possibility for confusion when wife and children travel and names don't match on passports or documents. Wife doesn't pass along surname to next generation, thereby propagating the injustice. Some junk mail may misidentify the wife as Mrs. [his name], and telemarketers also may ask to speak to Mrs. [his name], which may get increasingly irritating over time.

Full Faux Matriarchy

(Husband and kids take wife's surname, which really comes from her father, of course—thus the "faux.")

Pros: Everyone has same name. Wife's patriarchal surname gets passed down to next generation, breaking the cycle of only husbands' patriarchal surnames getting passed down. Husband may be praised as "enlightened" by other women. Husband gets chance at fresh start by losing unfortunate first/last combo (i.e., "Mike Litoris" becomes "Mike Wilson.")

Cons: Husband may be viewed as emasculated by other men. He has no way of referring to his original name because there's no male equivalent of maiden name ("master name?"). So he may have to refer to his original name as his maiden name, inviting ridicule. He also risks losing touch with his childhood friends, who can't find him without his maiden/master name.

Partial Faux Matriarchy

(Husband keeps his surname and kids take wife's surname.)

Pros: Wife's surname passed down.

Cons: Husband potentially feels estranged from rest of family.

Traditional Split Screen

(Daughters take wife's surname; sons take husband's surname.)

Pros: Everyone gets a little something.

Cons: Sons and daughters potentially feel estranged from each other. Endorses sexism in its arbitrary embrace of sex as name determinant. Fairness rationale falls apart if couple has only sons or only daughters and one parent gets stiffed.

Creative Split Screen

(Daughters take husband's surname; sons take wife's surname.)

Pros: Everyone gets a little something.

Cons: Might be viewed by others as weird, random, or stupid. Hard to explain to other adults without grinning sheepishly. Kids can't really explain it to other kids because it makes no sense—it doesn't even have a sexist rationale. Nobody does it.

First-Child Sex Dominant

(First child's sex determines which parent's surname gets chosen for that child and all subsequent children, regardless of sex—i.e., if first child is a daughter all children will have mother's surname and if a son all children will have father's surname.)

Pros: All children have same name.

Cons: Confusing to explain, inviting ridicule. Potential for estrangement for the losing parent.

Shoehorning

(Kids take either spouse's surname while other spouse's surname gets shoehorned in as a middle name or second middle name. Full disclosure: This is the route Cathi and I took. Our kids have Jones as their surname and Hanauer as their second middle name.)

Pros: Commonly done. Everyone gets a little something.

Cons: Ultimately weighted to one parent, whoever's name goes last. Still some confusion when traveling or making reservations. Possible estrangement for the spouse who gets shoehorned. Cathi complains that many forms for school or health care limit you to one middle name, meaning her last name, Hanauer, is the one most frequently left out.

Standard Hyphenation

(Combine both surnames as one last name, separated by a hyphen.)

Pros: Both spouses equally recognized (as long as they don't fight over name order).

Cons: Only a one-generation solution. The current wave of standard-hyphenation children will soon begin marrying en masse, many of them to other standard hyphenators, thereby triggering the triple-hyphenation snafu. How will it be resolved? We'll just have to wait and see.

Compound Hyphenation

(Combine already hyphenated surnames into one mega-hyphenated surname.)

Pros: Every parent's heritage is recognized for generations to come.

Cons: It's unsustainable.

Name Sharing

(Locating and marrying someone who already shares your surname.)

Pros: Total ease of transition into marriage. No problems with identification and family travel. No documents to change for anyone. Lively chatter at your wedding about the fun coincidence of shared surnames, where many guests on both sides of the aisle also will share that same name. Makes for a great story to tell new acquaintances for the rest of your lives. Might even get you some coverage in the local media.

Cons: Hard to pull off unless you have a really common name (like Jones!). Could lead to bad marriages that were formed simply because the couple was so eager to participate in name sharing they were blind to the reality of how mismatched they were in every other way.

Dicing and Splicing
(Cutting up both surnames into halves or pieces and reassembling them as a new name. In my family we might have become either "Jonauer" or "Hanes.")

Pros: Fair. Everyone shares same name.

Cons: Confusion/consternation among your friends and extended family, who may feel anything from amused to distraught by the change. Your extended family members who still have the old name might actually feel like you're rejecting them. What's more, the resulting hybrid name might prove to be a strange and one-of-a-kind moniker that makes you too easily Google-able, if you care about that.

For example, if Cathi and I had chosen to become "Jonauer," we would have been the only Google-able Jonauers in the world, though there is one person I found with the name "Jon Auer," who, according to Wikipedia, is "an American musician who cofounded the power pop band The Posies, along with Ken Stringfellow." See how easy that was? Now I could stalk him if I wanted to. But I digress. My point is this: if my wife and kids and I were to become the Jonauers, and any of us were to do something embarrassing or criminal, the world would have no trouble finding us on Facebook or Google Plus and defacing our "walls" with threats and ridicule, whereas with a name like Jones it's a little harder.

Wholesale Name Creation

(Creating a new name out of whatever you want, or to make a political point, like the professional basketball players known as "World B. Free" and "Metta World Peace.")

Pros: Bold. Shows everyone you're not afraid to make a statement (even a dumb one).

Cons: Forces people to call you a name that sounds unnatural, so instead they keep calling you by your old name, or they stop calling, period. Your kids might get teased at school, leading them to change their surname later on to something bland and common that attracts zero attention (like Jones!).

I'M SURE THERE ARE MANY MORE possibilities, but those thirteen choices ought to at least give you a place to start your discussions. And if, by the time your wedding day arrives, you *still* haven't been able to decide what name to go with, then why not turn over the decision to someone who is less likely to be troubled by the implications of the decision, like your dog?

That's what one couple did. Paralyzed with indecision over whether they should do Full Patriarchy or Full Faux Matriarchy, they put each of their last names on little signs in the lawn at their outdoor wedding. Then after they were pronounced hus-

band and wife, they let their dog loose, and the first name the
dog touched his nose to was the name they chose.

3. DEVISING A MORE EQUITABLE DIVISION OF LABOR BETWEEN SPOUSES

IN AN IDEAL world, couples wouldn't be reduced to bickering
about who is doing more in the marriage when it comes to housework, child care, and wage earning. Perhaps in the past couples
didn't have to argue as much about equitable division of labor
because the roles more commonly broke down along gender
lines. When husbands and wives weren't doing the same things,
the labor was not as monetarily comparable, so instead of spending their time arguing about who was doing more, couples of
previous generations were freed up to argue about other things.

By saying "not as monetarily comparable," I don't mean to
suggest one was more valuable than the other. It's just that the
man was typically coming home with a paycheck with a dollar
amount on it and the woman's contribution in the home was
harder to measure in a way that could be directly compared. It
has been said that you can't put a price on stay-at-home motherhood, though that hasn't stopped economists from trying. And
according to research conducted by Salary.com, today's average
stay-at-home mother would bring in about $115,000 a year if
she were to receive a paycheck for her efforts (a base salary of
$37,000 plus a whopping $78,000 in overtime)—an impressive
amount, to be sure.

Not only is that figure more than double the median family
income in the United States, it also happens to be more than

either Cathi or I earn in a typical year. If only we'd been paid in cash for all the cleaning and cooking and parenting we've done over the past two decades, our IRAs would be bursting!

Unfortunately, it's hard to count on that money when you're only talking about theoretical income, which is hard to deposit in a bank, unlike a physical paycheck, which is real money you can buy stuff with. But today most married couples have dual incomes (aka "dueling" incomes), which means they have hard numbers to work with. Your income is a specific number, and the hours you've spent doing chores and child care is a specific number, too, if you care to add them up. You've both got hard data with which to fight and bargain, should you choose to do so.

Granted, not many couples sit down with a spreadsheet and compare earnings and chores and child care and then hash out an exact fifty–fifty split. But these kinds of calculations are being factored into marriages in ways large and small. Husbands and wives want it to be fair. Gay couples want it to be fair. And it will lead to conflict if either spouse believes it isn't.

Romantics might argue that truly loving someone means caring more about your spouse's happiness than your own. Which is a nice thought, but in reality people who care more about their spouse's happiness than their own might start to feel taken advantage of after a while if their spouse doesn't act selfless in the exact same amount. Besides, where do we draw the line with such selflessness? If it makes my wife happy to buy a new Ferrari and use it to have sex with strangers in parking garages, and I care more about her happiness than my own, then technically I ought to cheer her on if I truly love her.

But after a certain point my sense of self-worth might start to take a hit. Because if she truly loved me, she would notice that her behavior was making me unhappy. And if she cared more about my happiness than her own, she would then stop having random sex in parking garages, sell the Ferrari, and use the proceeds to fly us to Bali for a romantic getaway.

Preaching selflessness in marriage isn't the answer. Pursuing fairness is. The good news is that we are making progress in this regard. A recent Pew Research survey showed that overall hours worked between fathers and mothers in dual-income households—a combination of paid work, housework, and child care—has almost reached parity: fifty-nine hours a week for mothers and fifty-eight hours for fathers. Fathers outpaced mothers in paid work, logging an average of eleven more hours a week than their wives (forty-two to thirty-one). But mothers erased that difference (and then some) by putting in seven more hours of housework every week (sixteen to nine) and five more hours of child care (twelve to seven). Those gaps, too, have been steadily narrowing.

How will you do it in your marriage? How adaptable will you be to change? If you're already married and have been dealing with these thorny issues, how might you alter your current arrangement to work better? Please discuss.

To facilitate, I offer some popular options below. While it may be true that every family is as unique as a snowflake, the options they face in this regard seem to come from a standardized list, not unlike choosing a health-care plan where you are limited to the same three "Freedom" plans, none of which are even remotely about freedom. So it is with our available plans for the division of earning and household labor. Like an insurance company, I can put a positive spin on the names. But in the end they are what they are: a muddle.

A brief explanation: the only plans I include are those with the ebb and flow of constant horse-trading, where both spouses have paying jobs and do housework and child care, simply because these are the thorniest and what I hear people struggling with the most. Those marriages with stay-at-home moms and working dads and the rarer (but growing) arrangements with stay-at-home dads and working moms are hardly conflict-free, but the roles at least seem more cleanly split and the marriages don't seem to be as prone to constant comparison and negotiation as the more mixed-up arrangements.

Progressive Equality Plan (Gender Blind)

In this perfect choice for high-achieving idealists, both parents will strive to work about the same amount at their day jobs, earn roughly the same income at those jobs, and do housework, shopping, cooking, and child care in roughly equal amounts. This also is the ideal choice for fathers and mothers who hope to teach their children, via gender-blind modeling, that there is no such thing as "men's work" and "women's work," because both parents will rotate among the various home and child-care duties and are expected to be skilled and knowledgeable in all areas.

Fathers will be expected to produce their children's shoe sizes, medication prescriptions, and the names of their kindergarten teachers on demand, and mothers won't think twice about firing up the snowblower or taking a sledgehammer to the Sheetrock.

Pros: Totally fair. Children can feel liberated to pursue any career and perform any chore without all that ugly sexist baggage.

Cons: In today's economy of shifting jobs and layoffs and

demotions, the fragile balance can be hard to maintain. Rather than specialize in bill paying or snowblowing, you must each become a Renaissance parent, mastering all chores and responsibilities inside the house and out, and this will take time you don't have. So while you're both trying to learn TurboTax and where to find gluten on food labels instead of splitting up those tasks, your kids may languish, unloved and unattended.

Retro Equality Plan (Gender Aware)

The Retro Equality Plan serves as a great option for those who seek basic equality in wage earning, housework, and child care but don't care much about (or aren't able to handle) having a gender-blind rotation of household chores.

Couples who begin with Progressive Equality and later downgrade to this plan may be well-intended moms and dads who earnestly tried to switch up the roles but found it just didn't work: Dad's cooking tasted like rawhide and salt, and Mom's lawn mowing was ravaging the tulip bed and ruining her best boots. Other couples drawn to this plan may include those who happen to really enjoy their traditional male and female roles and responsibilities and don't believe they're harming their children by reinforcing sexist stereotypes. Or maybe they may secretly believe there *is* such a thing as "men's work" and "women's work" and hope to raise kids who feel the same way.

Pros: Fair division of labor, as long as the household division is acceptable to both. Saves time because you don't have to master the whole slate of household chores, which is time you can then spend with your children.

Cons: Your brain withers as you fail to learn new skills. Your empathy drains away as you remain in your comfortable rut and cease walking in your spouse's shoes. Reinforces sexist stereotypes, possibly limiting your children's horizons. Scorn from gender-blind peers who consider you and your kind to be an obstacle to progress.

Freedom Flex Plan (Gender Blind or Gender Aware)

With the Freedom Flex Plan, accommodations are made to account for large disparities in income as well as availability for household chores and child care. Rather than obsessing over earning the same amount and dividing the chores and child care fifty–fifty, participants in this plan adjust as needed based on factors on the ground, who's earning more and less, and who has more time. So if Spouse A gets a job that pays $80,000 a year, and Spouse B is able to pull in $40,000, then Spouse B will do x percent more housework and child care to account for the disparity in income.

This arrangement can work well if Spouse A earns that extra income by working longer hours than Spouse B. But one complication faced by couples in this plan is when one spouse's income doesn't reflect the hours worked. If Spouse A earns $80,000 by working full-time while Spouse B earns $40,000 by also working full-time, or if Spouse B is even working *longer* hours while being paid far less overall (due to economic factors beyond his or her control), then should Spouse B still be expected to scrub extra pans and get less sleep while Spouse A snoozes away, just because B's skills aren't as rewarded as A's? That's a tough one.

The Freedom Flex Plan, by the way, can be "Progressive" or "Retro" in dividing household responsibilities. When it comes to this, Cathi and I mostly subscribe to the Retro option, I'm embarrassed to admit. We've been satisfied with the Freedom Flex Plan overall, each having been the top earner at different phases in our lives, and neither of us has ever been 100 percent earner or homemaker.

Yet Cathi does most of the cooking, shopping, and planning, and also devotes more time and energy to the children than I do. And I mostly handle the cars, bills, outdoor grilling of meat, home repair, and yard work.

Pros: You can constantly adjust the balance as jobs change, income varies, and household demands shift.

Cons: You must constantly adjust the balance as jobs change, income varies, and household demands shift.

CHAPTER REVIEW AND CHECKLIST

How will you maintain individuality in your marriage?
(Check all that apply)

    ☐ Keep separate houses
    ☐ Act a little divorced
    ☐ Have open marriage
    ☐ Acquire office spouse
    ☐ Other _____ (please explain)

How will you create a fairer family name?
(Choose only one)

    ☐ Full Patriarchy (this one is not fairer, by the way)
    ☐ Partial Patriarchy (not much fairer either)
    ☐ Full Faux Matriarchy
    ☐ Partial Faux Matriarchy
    ☐ Traditional Split Screen
    ☐ Creative Split Screen (not recommended)
    ☐ First-Child Sex Dominant
    ☐ Shoehorning (recommended)
    ☐ Standard Hyphenation
    ☐ Compound Hyphenation (not recommended)
    ☐ Name Sharing (highly recommended)
    ☐ Dicing and Splicing
    ☐ Wholesale Name Creation
    ☐ Other _____ (Please explain)

How will you devise a more equitable division of labor?
(Choose only one)

    ☐ Progressive Equality Plan
    ☐ Retro Equality Plan
    ☐ Freedom Flex Plan
    ☐ Other _____ (Please explain)

You are now free to move on to the next stage of your life.

7

Monotony

WHEN MARRIAGE IS A WHEELBARROW

WHAT'S THE BEST WAY TO REDISCOVER passion in marriage once monogamy has morphed into monotony, intimacy has constricted into claustrophobia, and familiarity has bred contempt? I wish I had the answer, because clearly millions of people would like to know. And I suspect they've already spent billions trying to find out.

The stories I receive often ask questions—not directly but implicitly—and two questions dominate. First, from the young: "How do I find love?" And second, from those struggling through the marital malaise of midlife: "How do I get it back?"

Of course, it's not really love they want back so much as attention, excitement, and passion. If passion is the fleeting bloom that launched the relationship, then marriage is the sturdy wheelbarrow left behind in passion's wake. Many wind up feeling so disappointed or even cheated by this tradeoff they decide to shove their marital wheelbarrow into a ditch, often by uttering brain-dead lines to their spouse like: "I still love you. I'm just not *in love* with you."

Translated from the original bullshit, that excuse roughly reads: "Although I value the role you've played in my life, you've come to bore me."

And there's no denying it—marriage can get boring. It's full of mind-numbing routines, cyclical arguments, perfunctory sex, and repetitive conversations. In my own twenty-year marriage, my wife has a habit of asking me to do something and then saying, "You're not going to forget, are you? Just tell me now if you're going to forget so I know I'll have to do it myself."

And I'll say (for the hundredth time), "I can't know in advance if I'm going to forget. That's not how forgetting works."

"Just tell me," she'll say.

Granted, there's much to appreciate about the familiarity and continuity of long-term relationships. A shared history is a wonderful thing. The routines and traditions of family life can bring comfort, joy, tax advantages, and a longer life span. And we've also got that standard-issue promise of our golden years to look forward to—sitting on the porch swing together, sipping decaffeinated Earl Grey tea as the sun sets, etc.

That's all great. Wouldn't trade it for the world! But the lack of passion among longtime married couples is a pervasive, intractable, and often relationship-ending problem. And it seems there's no avoiding it.

Among my fifty thousand strangers, I've heard from only a handful of couples who claim to have maintained sexually charged marriages through the decades. And the one story I published from this happier-than-thou crowd, by the writer

Ayelet Waldman about her still-sexy marriage (with four children) to Pulitzer Prize–winning hubby Michael Chabon, was met with jeers and hostility when she went on *Oprah* to talk about it, mostly because she dared to confess that she puts her marriage ahead of motherhood.

That alignment of priorities, she explained, is part of what has allowed her to keep her marriage passionate over the years. And she argued that doing so is also a healthier model for children, most of whom would be better off with a little less time in mommy's spotlight, especially if it means being raised by loving, affectionate parents instead of resentful, bickering ones.

As she spoke, the studio audience, which appeared to be mostly composed of young and midlife mothers (along with a smattering of befuddled-looking husbands), regarded her as though she were some two-headed alien from another planet.

She might as well have been, given how rare her kind of marriage is these days. In fact, the majority of us seem to spend our days dutifully pushing our wheelbarrows through the rut of midlife while feeling more than a little unappreciated by our spouses. Huge numbers of us are also flirting with and fantasizing about old flames on Facebook and other social media venues, wishing we could have affairs without consequences, and—as we race off to meet that blast from the past who makes our heart pound—asking ourselves the same question from the starter quiz: Why shouldn't we be allowed to feel this kind of passion again after so many years of not feeling it, even if it means going outside of the marriage to get it?

Try asking that of Oprah's studio audience. Their response surely would be swift and deafening: "BOO!!!"

Talk-show-audience puritanism aside, though, it's a good

question. If we aren't lucky enough to be among those five or six (okay, maybe thirty) couples worldwide who are able to effortlessly maintain sexual potency throughout marriage and parenthood, what are our choices? To quash our unfulfilled desires and simply resign ourselves to the limitations of marriage? To sneak around trying to get our needs met elsewhere? To confront the issue head-on and work together to try to restore the passion in our relationship?

Yes, yes, and yes. Basically, if we don't want to get divorced and start all over again, those are our choices: quashing, sneaking, or restoring.

THOSE WHO QUASH

PEOPLE WHO QUASH their unfulfilled desires have decided to accept their marriage for what it is and just want to figure out how to feel okay about it. As you might guess, this approach involves a process of near-constant rationalization. Rather than waste their energy trying to figure out how to get their needs met, quashers choose to waste their energy rationalizing why they shouldn't even try.

Oh well, they tell themselves, *so we're never going to be all hot for each other like we used to be. I've still got a lot to be thankful for. If I had it to do all over again, I wouldn't change a thing. I love my spouse and my family. I love my life. I love my dogs and house and garden. What's a little shallow physical pleasure and attention compared to all that? Things could be a lot worse, that's for sure. Sex is overrated anyway. At least it gave me my kids. When you think about it, what else do you really need it for?*

This energetic cheerfulness may spill over into other aspects of their life as well. On Facebook, those who quash will tend to post upbeat entries about family vacations and career advancements and children's accomplishments, along with a healthy dose of cute YouTube video links and inspiring aphorisms about how to find joy in everyday life.

These postings might lead some of their Facebook friends to dismiss them as being in total denial, but they aren't, not really. They just don't see the point of wallowing in self-pity when they have accomplished everything they hoped to—marriage, family, career—and by all accounts are living the dream. So they aren't having wild sex every day or every week or even once a month (or ever). Big deal! It goes with the territory. Grow up. Life means choices. You can't have everything. Be grateful for what you do have, and get over yourself.

Not all quashers are the same, of course. As with all personality types, there's a spectrum. And the quashing spectrum runs the gamut from the bitterly resigned to the appreciatively so. Those who are bitterly resigned tend to be harshly judgmental of anyone who doesn't share their grim acceptance and defeatism. They will scorn those who cheat or divorce as being self-centered sluts or sex addicts who can't keep their pants on. They will deride those who escape into Internet porn as being mentally impaired deviants (even while sampling it on their own when no one is looking). They will express concern for the children of divorce even as they privately cheer the competitive advantage they believe the stability of their union gives their own children over the damaged detritus of broken homes.

The bitterly resigned will not go to couples counseling because, well, what's the point? Stuff like that is for privileged whiners. Anyway, what are we supposed to say? Boo hoo—life isn't as fun as it used to be? We hardly need to pay someone for that.

The bitterly resigned won't try to spice up their marriage by experimenting sexually because it's just too embarrassing—all that talk of "role-playing" and "positions" and "gratification" and "pleasure." Yuck. It's just not normal.

They won't have affairs because they prize loyalty (and martyrdom) and don't want to hurt their spouse or children or humiliate themselves in the community. Only weak people who can't keep their pants on do that.

As far as the example this kind of relationship sets, I hear from adult children of the bitterly resigned all the time. They're typically the ones struggling to reconcile the societal pressure they feel to get married with their deeply ingrained aversion to the institution. Although they have no more trouble finding love than anybody else, they fear the grind that love might turn into if they were to marry. They will say things like, "My parents' marriage is not exactly something I'd hope to replicate."

I'm no doctor, but based on anecdotal evidence I would guess that feeling bitterly resigned about your marriage is not good for your health. If someone were to conduct a medical survey of such couples, I wouldn't be surprised if they were to find high rates of heart disease, cancer, and obesity among this population, because all that emotional suppression has got to take a physical toll, doesn't it?

What a difference a spectrum can make, though, because those at the other end of the quashing range—the appreciatively resigned—seem to be among the healthiest and happiest married people alive. Not much sexual passion, if any, left in the marriage? No problem. Like Dr. Seuss's Whos down in Who-ville, who merrily hold hands and sing after being robbed on Christmas Eve of all their food and possessions, the appreciatively resigned rise each morning not dwelling on their marital shortfalls but counting their mutual blessings, whatever they may be: a shared sense of humor, an exchange of kind gestures, the enthusiastic pursuit of a common interest. Somehow over time they have managed to grow together rather than apart. And they remain engaged and connected despite having to face and work through the same challenges and disappointments that any long-term relationship must if it is to endure.

Observing such marriages from the outside, you may start to feel like the Grinch on his mountaintop shivering in the snow, mystified by the resilience of the Whos down below:

Why, they feel happy while aging and when their sex lags!

They're content when his dick droops and when her chest sags!

It's enough to make you puzzle till your puzzler is sore.

Until you think of something you hadn't before:

Perhaps marriage, to them, doesn't feel like a chore.

Maybe marriage, in their case, means a little bit more.

THOSE WHO SNEAK

THOSE WHO SNEAK do not feel the impulse to rationalize away their desires, nor are they content to quash them. Instead, they try to figure out how to get their needs met elsewhere. Not by cheating or otherwise jeopardizing the marriage (we'll talk about the cheaters and jeopardizers in the next chapter). No, those who sneak merely redirect their passion away from the marriage, into pursuits and distractions and flirtations that entertain and titil-late but fall short of all-out betrayal. This last part is very im-portant, because sneakers do not like an emotional mess. This is the very reason they can't face the issues more directly in their marriage, because they don't deal well with confrontation. So they will try to avoid taking things too far in their sneaking ac-tivities, even if sometimes, in the end, they can't help themselves.

As a matter of convenience, much of their sneaking will be conducted online. Sneakers are never without their electronic devices. When sitting, they will almost always be staring into an open laptop or e-tablet, even if they're already watching TV. And while walking or driving or cooking or doing chores, they'll be staring into a smartphone. As a dodge, they might complain about how the demands of work follow them everywhere, but in truth only a tiny fraction of what they're doing is work. The rest is all boredom alleviation.

For this kind of gadgetry-obsessed type, the hardest work of marriage is listening. To their spouses they'll mutter "What?" and "Say again?" constantly, but then they won't listen when the question or instruction is repeated either and are too em-barrassed to say "What?" a second or third time, meaning that they'll never know what was said. If it's important, they figure, they'll find out eventually. Like when they fail to pick up their daughter at dance class and she texts "WTF?" Or when the smoke alarm starts blaring over the stove they didn't know they were supposed to turn off.

Sneakers these days have so many temptations and ways to escape that you'd have to say this is the golden age of sneaking, though the way things are headed with communications technology it seems it can only get more golden going forward until we plateau in an orgy of gadget-enabled perma-cheating.

For now, let's examine a few of today's more common behaviors.

People You May Know

Sneakers will log a lot of hours on Facebook, many of which will be spent stalking old flames from high school and college, or anyone else they find remotely attractive. They love being prompted by the "People You May Know" feature to check out friends of friends, because sneakers always want to "know" more people and usually aren't bold enough to flirt with people they don't know. This is why an old flame is the perfect target.

Have you ever received a friend request from a long-ago love or acquaintance or schoolmate who very early on in your "Hey, how've you been?" messaging session either asks leading questions about the state of your marriage or confesses to loneliness or boredom in his or her own? If so, you've been targeted by a sneaker.

The standard routine that leads from initial contact to messaging flirtation to possible in-person meeting is so yawningly predictable I can hardly write about it here without putting myself to sleep, but I'll try.

After an opening exchange of how-you-dos, the sneaker will launch right in. . . .

SNEAKER: yeah im married 2 but i dont know. we kind of do our own thing these days. what about u?
TARGET: lol i know how that is.

SNEAKER: do u really?

TARGET: omg who doesnt

SNEAKER: u and me used to have so much fun partying right?

TARGET: yeah like 100 yrs ago lol.

SNEAKER: we should try to hang out sometime. get together 4 lunch or whatevs.

TARGET: omg that would be so crazy to c u again.

SNEAKER: how far away are u? like 3 hrs?

TARGET: yeah. long drive for just lunch lol!

SNEAKER: so do u really do ur own thing in ur marriage, too?

TARGET: LMAO!!! OMG U HAVENT CHANGED AT ALL!!!!!

SNEAKER: so is that a yes? uh oh gotta go. ball & chain in room.

TARGET: ok. c u l8ter ;)

Will they actually get together for lunch? And if they do get together and they have a great time—then what? Will they A) rekindle their romance, and B) decide to divorce their spouses, and C) marry each other and live happily ever after?

Um, probably not. Needless to say, the complexity and emotional toll involved in actually getting from point A to point C in this fantasy is staggering. Yet this kind of Facebook-inspired daydreaming ("If only I could be with _____, I'd be so much happier and more sexually fulfilled") is among the most common dilemmas I hear expressed by bored married people.

And it seems to be the quintessential quandary of those who sneak, as they ask themselves time and again: *How can I pursue this passion without ruining my life? How can I get something without losing anything? There must be a way!*

But there isn't a way.

There must be!

Eventually the bloom on this kind of fantasy may fade, sometimes sooner rather than later, when the crush starts to irritate or simply grow stale. But the "grass is greener" allure is a dream that dies hard. And even as one fantasy withers, a new one sprouts in its place. Not typically as greener grass but, you know, as another weed.

Lunching with Porn Stars

Sneakers who need a sexual distraction but don't trust themselves with any level of actual human interaction often find a perfect match in the world of online pornography.

One personality trait that must be prominent among sneakers is the ability to compartmentalize, to wall off the various parts of their personality into hermetically sealed units. They need to feel that their sneaking is like scratching an itch—nothing more and nothing less. And once they've scratched that itch, they can then return to the world of Legos and dirty dishes and homework assistance refreshed and ready.

And to the sneaker, nothing quite screams "compartmentalize" more than being able to watch a whips-and-chains anal-sex romp on their laptop while their kids play Chutes and Ladders a few feet away. If the kids invite the sneaking parent to play Chutes and Ladders with them, all the parent has to do is snap shut the laptop and, voilà, the sneaker has gone from bondage voyeur to engaged role model in seconds, no strings attached.

And unlike with Facebook flirtations, no matter how much a sneaker may fantasize about how much better his sex life would be if he were dating a porn star, he can't actually track down any porn stars to ask them if they'd like to get together for lunch. Not that I haven't heard from at least one sneaker who tried. But in the end he couldn't find her. Not that he tried very hard. Because what would he have done if he did?

THOSE WHO RESTORE

WHEN THEIR MARRIAGE starts to feel subpar, those who are inclined to try to restore the passion will sit down and have a frank, sensible discussion about where their marriage is and where they would like it to be. Unlike sneakers, a restorer's instinct is to turn toward the marriage, not away from it. Together the couple will set goals and then seek the means to achieve those goals. Typically affluent, educated, successful, and highly motivated, restorer couples almost single-handedly support the vast and profitable marriage-improvement industry.

To figure out how to proceed, they'll do what they've always done when faced with a thorny problem: conduct extensive research on the topic and then come up with a plan of action. And it won't take long before they find out that, ironically, the most recommended strategies for reigniting passion in one's marriage—passion that has waned in part due to the deadening weight of its routines—involves loading up the relationship with even more routines, albeit of an ostensibly restorative nature: date nights, couples counseling, dance classes, scheduled sex, ten for tens (committing to ten hugs of at least ten seconds in

duration every single day), Fresh Flower Fridays (a boon to the
local florist, if not your marriage), required kisses upon parting,
lunchtime exchanges of erotic texts or e-mails, and possibly some
creative midday play at the local Holiday Inn involving nipple
clamps, silk scarves, and an eye patch.

Drudgery and Spice

The restorative activities undertaken by such couples can be divided into two groups: drudgery and spice. The drudgery, like
research and couples counseling, is supposed to be hard work,
whereas the spice, such as erotic e-mails, "creative" play, and
kisses upon parting, is supposed to be fun and sexy. Depending on a couple's proclivities, however, the drudgery may actually turn out to be fun (like reading to each other in bed from
marriage-improvement books) and the attempts at spice may
start to feel more like work (sitting silently through yet another
date night when you can't think of anything to say to each other,
or having to get out of the car and go back inside because you yet
again forgot your required parting kiss).

These attempts at relighting the flame may actually (mi-
raculously) work for some couples, but for many others they
seem to be less about having fun or feeling sexy or "rediscovering" each other than they are about demonstrating a nose-to-
the-grindstone determination that the couple is willing to try
anything to stay together and remain vital, which can have a
bonding appeal of its own. After all, you've got quite a lot going
for you if you're willing to commit to having a weekly drink
in a bar together when you'd rather be at home watching *Mad
Men*, or learning the fox-trot when you hate dancing, or giving

up your cherished Saturday-morning run to partake in a regular bedroom session of holding hands naked while staring into each other's eyes (and seeing where that leads).

Like at-risk teens who are kept off the streets and headed in a positive direction through after-school sports or Big Brother and Big Sister programs, restorer couples who embrace these new routines are also kept out of other people's beds and focused on healthier alternatives, safely sequestered with each other in constructive environments and away from the slippery slope of online social networking and the seductive allure of karaoke nights with colleagues.

What's more, if you're an overachieving restorer couple (and there's actually no such thing as an underachieving restorer couple), you'll want to be able to say you tried everything possible to improve your marriage. So essentially it's just a matter of going down the list and checking everything off. And a big-ticket item on that list, one of the first they will eagerly pursue, is couples counseling.

And How Does That Make You Feel?

Restorer couples typically will find a marital therapist by asking their individual therapists to recommend someone who might best help them with their joint issues. At their first session, they'll feel liberated to unload about their various disappointments in the same way they've been doing in individual therapy, except in this case the person they're talking about is sitting right next to them. And after they've finished their explaining and blaming and venting, the therapist will turn to the object of their frustration and say, "And how does that make you feel?"

The answer will be: "Not very good."

When they leave, it's likely neither of them will feel very good. They will have all kinds of new issues and understandings to work through and to talk about at the next session, and the next, which they will do. And afterward, months later, although they may know each other better, and even get along better, their new knowledge, alas, probably will not make them want to rush home and have sex with one another.

The only exception was one couple I heard from whose therapist said, partway into their very first session, "What you guys need to do is go home right now and have sex. Go on. Get out of here. Go have sex."

So they did. And it was good. Once.

And that was the problem with that particular approach—it can only work one time. By the next visit, the couple was onto him. And they didn't want to pay someone a lot of money to tell them to go home and have sex when they were fully capable of doing that on their own. Except they weren't doing that on their own. Thus the conundrum.

Marital-Boredom Scholarship

Every restorer couple ultimately will want to become marital-boredom scholars, to read everything they can get their hands on that explains why living and having sex with the same person for twenty or thirty years can get boring and what to do about it when it happens to you. And in their pursuit of such knowledge, they will convert their bedside nightstands from leisure-reading podiums scattered with travel magazines and suspense novels into social-science libraries stacked with ominous-sounding book titles such as:

I Don't
Should I Stay or Go?
Marriage Shock
The Weekend Marriage
The Meaning of Wife
For Better, For Worse
The Female Brain
Mating in Captivity

And those are just a sampling from *one* woman's social-science library (my wife's, in fact).

From these books and others, restorers will learn how their boredom may ebb and flow and even intensify in the coming years before it finally levels off into the pleasant hum of old age. They'll become experts in the ways marriage has oppressed human beings throughout history and in the reasons men and women have driven each other crazy for all of eternity.

They'll be schooled in the mechanics of orgasms and the ravages of menopause and be reminded that fighting the body's decline is hopeless but that doesn't mean they still can't have fun in bed with their lifelong soul mate if they take advantage of the element of surprise and wear costumes.

They'll be convinced of the ways in which Homo sapiens are like bonobos in how frequently and randomly we like to have casual sex. And they'll be persuaded that a series of mistaken assumptions about evolution and our origins have made us all basket cases when it comes to experiencing lifelong sexual fulfillment without succumbing to ruinous guilt and shame. They may come away from their scholarship believing that monogamy is only for the repressed and deluded, that traditional male and female roles are crushing yet inescapable, and that marriage is doomed for everyone except for those who are willing to cover their eyes, plug their ears, deny reality, and live in an emotional straitjacket for the rest of their lives.

By the end of their self-study, restorers will have discussed all of these concepts in bed with their spouses (instead of having sex) and may be questioning whether their efforts to fix the problem will actually pay off. They will have hugged and kissed and danced and date-nighted until they can hug and kiss and dance and date-night no more. And although they will have had some good times that made them remember why they fell in love in the first place, they won't exactly have turned back the clock in terms of reclaiming that ever-elusive "passion."

Inevitably, as the intellectually curious people they are, restorers will return to their original and most perplexing questions: *How much do we have a right to expect from marriage? Is this simply as good as it gets? We do care about each other. We don't fight too much. We love our kids. Health is generally good. We have no right to complain, really. We're still among the most privileged creatures this earth has ever hosted. Can't we just be happy with what we have? And isn't there a risk that in pressing for more we'll turn something pretty good into something really bad?*

You can see how even the most ambitious restorer couple might eventually pull back on all the improvement techniques and join the ranks of the appreciatively resigned. Which isn't such a bad thing. After all, as appreciatively resigned couples say to themselves nearly every day, "There are worse things, right?"

There are worse things. In fact, you can read about a few of them in the very next chapter.

8

Infidelity

IS THIS WRONG?

NOT LONG AGO I READ A story about a woman's secretive relationship with a man who was soon to be married. Their mutual steaminess involved days of emoticon-filled e-chatting, nights of sexy texting, an occasional dinner out, and a lot of naked Skyping. The vast majority of their relationship was online flirtation and video play; only occasionally did they get together in person, and never for sex, just for minor-league, in-public, under-the-table groping.

This man supposedly loved his fiancée, but he also loved having plenty of naughty fun with his e-mistress. He didn't want to have to give up one for the other, not as his wedding drew closer, and not even, he hoped, after he was married. Yet when he stopped giggling and fondling himself long enough to look at the situation with some perspective, he would ask his e-mistress (via the chat box, while staring at her nudity on the laptop cam), "Is this wrong?"

The e-mistress didn't want to judge. Wasn't the rightness or wrongness of this for him to figure out? And wasn't it also his job to do something about it if he felt the need? After all, she didn't have a fiancé or even anyone else she was seeing at the time. *She* wasn't the one who was cheating.

Then again, neither was he, technically. At least not according to the rules of infidelity that say cheating means having sex with one person while being married to another, because he wasn't married (yet) and he and his e-mistress weren't having sex (yet). Even so, with all of their secrecy, on-screen nudity, in-person touching, and sexy online banter (including on the morning of his wedding), they clearly were gathering speed on an especially steep downward slope of the infidelity highway. But if you were to measure their sexual shenanigans on the Department of Homeland Security's color-coded scale for level of marital threat, how high would it rate? Yellow for "elevated"? Orange for "high"?

When it comes to infidelity, people want to know where they stand in terms of how "wrong" their behavior is or how guilty they should feel. They want to know which lines they may have crossed and where those lines are. And they want to know how they should view themselves: as weak and all too human (preferred), or as selfish and narcissistic (not preferred)?

It can be hard to get definitive answers to any of these questions. In the stories I've seen, the relative "wrongness" of infidelity seems to be very much in the eye of the philanderer (and the philandered upon) and can encompass a wide range of behavior from merely being attracted to someone other than your spouse or partner, to engaging in simultaneous affairs, to being secretly involved in multiple families at once. The only constant is deceit. And as with everything else, technology has only added to our menu of possibilities.

Some consider their partner watching online porn a form of cheating. In one fraught tale I read, a woman was agonizing about having caught her husband "cheating" yet again and lamenting how this time it was going to spell the end of their marriage. I kept expecting to hear about all the sleeping around he'd been doing, but it quickly became clear that he hadn't been sleeping around at all: he'd been looking at porn again on his laptop after promising not to.

For others, public exposure and humiliation may be a major factor in how they view infidelity. For example, if their partner flirts audaciously at a neighborhood cocktail party in a way that friends notice and mention in whispered asides, they might consider that a worse offense than if their partner were to have a one-night sexual encounter on a business trip that their friends would never hear about.

If you're the one doing the cheating, your conscience will likely speak up and tell you when you're doing something your partner might have a problem with, and then it's up to you to decide whether or not you want to listen to that voice. If you know you've crossed the line and choose to keep your behavior secret, you'll probably try to justify your behavior to yourself and eventually, perhaps, to others.

Love is full of rationalizations and justifications, but few situations bring out the hairsplitting lawyer in us as much as infidelity. Since so many of us will at some point either fully cheat, kind of cheat, or almost cheat, it's worth pulling together a few of the more popular rationalizations and defenses in a handy guide so when the time comes and you have some urgent justifying to do, you're not left scrambling. After all, when you're cheating (or trying to figure out if your behavior qualifies), you've probably got a lot on your plate already. Here are the approaches I see cheaters grappling with and embracing most often.

1. HUMAN BEINGS ARE NOT NATURALLY MONOGAMOUS ANYWAY

CHEATERS WITH A background in science or who have studied up on the issue might argue that having sex with a lot of people throughout our lives (or at the same time) is what human beings are meant to do; it's programmed into our DNA. We can try to act civilized and responsible and cram all those wayward yearnings into a lockbox and throw away the key, but doing so means we're fighting our own biology.

Just look at the rest of the animal kingdom. Hardly any other animals mate with only one partner for life, and most of the ones that do aren't exactly creatures you'd want to be associated with. A brief list includes:

- jumping rats
- black vultures
- anglerfish (in which the male is faithful only because he is *fused* to the female as a source of sperm)
- *Diplozoon paradoxum* (a tapeworm that lives in the intestines of a fish; males and females are also fused together until death)
- *Schistosoma mansoni* (a human parasitic worm, in which the female lives within the male's "canal")

Admittedly, not all monogamous animals can be so easily dismissed as creepy or otherwise unappealing, especially when you consider that bald eagles, our celebrated national bird, are monogamous for life. And emperor penguins, among the most beloved creatures on earth, are at least serially monogamous, standing by each other for a full mating season. Emperor penguins are also admirably egalitarian during breeding and egg tending, with the male taking responsibility for sitting on the couple's egg to keep it warm and protected while the female ventures off for two months of swimming and eating.

You might think the males would get antsy from sixty-four straight days of egg sitting while also fasting in temperatures as low as negative forty degrees Fahrenheit and winds as high as ninety miles per hour. You'd think if anyone could be tempted into some inappropriate sexual activity to break up the coldness, starvation, and boredom it would be a male emperor penguin during egg-sitting duty. But does he decide to leave his egg behind to cruise the colony for a steamy encounter with an alluring female, as many human males would if they were stuck in a similarly grim situation? No.

Still, it must be said that bald eagles and emperor penguins are birds, and as much as we may admire them, we simply don't have much in common with birds. As the mammals we are, descended from apes, we have more in common with nature's horniest of horndogs, the bonobo chimpanzee (formerly known as the pygmy chimpanzee—curiously, as they are not small). Bonobos are so highly sexualized they are known to have sex while greeting, sex when parting, sex for healing, sex to encourage peace, and sex for any other conceivable reason. They have sex in almost as many creative positions as humans do. In fact, they are the only nonhumans known to have face-to-face sex, to French kiss, and to have oral sex. And they are so crazily nonmonogamous they will have sex with just about any other bonobo within reach—only mothers and sons seem to steer clear of each other sexually.

According to the evolutionary justification, this is how a lot of us human beings would act if we hadn't been stuffed into this monogamy straitjacket and instead were allowed to bust out and embrace our true bonobo nature. Or so argue Christopher Ryan and Cacilda Jethá in their book *Sex at Dawn*, which you should probably read if you want to justify your infidelity by embracing such theories.

And this brings up the greatest challenge for anyone relying upon a scientific and evolutionary approach: it will require a fair amount of reading and research, something you probably don't have time for. *Sex at Dawn* is fascinating, but it's more than four hundred pages long, and that's only one source. You'll need to digest several if you want to build a case that's strong enough to convince yourself that what you're doing not only is fine but practically a biological imperative.

Yet even if you become an expert on the subject, you still need to be careful with this approach, because no matter how compelling such scientific blather may sound in an academic sense, it can come across as a little cold to a weeping spouse who feels utterly betrayed and whose reaction to your excuse might involve telling you exactly where you can shove your evolutionary rationalizations (as in, right up your bonobo).

2. WE SHOULD BE ALLOWED TO FEEL PASSION IN OUR LIVES

ADVOCATES OF THIS approach will argue that pleasure is good. Pleasure should be pursued. Why would our Founding Fathers have championed the pursuit of happiness if they wanted everyone to rot away in sex-starved relationships, passing up opportunities for encounters with people who might bring them pleasure? What could make anyone happier than feeling loved and sexually fulfilled? Infidelity may get a bad rap for its destabilizing effects on marriage and society, but when you strip away all the alarmist language about "betrayal" and "broken vows" and "violating the sanctity" of things, what do you really have other than two people pursuing pleasure in ways that bring them happiness?

As "passion" advocates like to tell themselves, "You only live once" (aka YOLO). You have one life, and then that's it, you're dead. And after you marry, it's sex with only one person for a bunch of decades, and then you're dead. And if that person isn't as interested in having sex as you are, or isn't interested in having sex with *you*, then it's going to be just you having sex with yourself until you're dead, or no sex at all; it's up to you.

Not to imply that the end of your sex life is necessarily the end of the world (though it could lead to the end of the species if more broadly embraced). Some people stop liking sex as much as they get older, and don't miss it. Others never did like it. But for those who still do like it, having none for the rest of their lives is not okay. As any passionate person will tell you, a life without passion is no life at all.

If the voice running through your head sounds anything like that, then cheating—should the opportunity present itself—will sound more and more justifiable. You might even be able to convince yourself that it's more pathetic *not* to have affairs than to have them.

3. TECHNICALLY, I WASN'T UNFAITHFUL

SEX USED TO be easier to define; now there are a whole slew of activities that are "sex-like" but not actual sex, including avatar sex and Skype sex, as previously discussed. Given the range of ways we can be sexual and loving with another person these days without being in physical contact or even in the same room, what does it mean anymore to be unfaithful?

Those with a legal sensibility are able to find endless wiggle room when facing the question of whether or not they're being unfaithful. They view infidelity as being a kind of court case, where they are innocent until proven guilty. They tend to see the world through that narrow lens already, as a place of loopholes to take advantage of for personal gain. And they justify their infidelity—both to themselves, and, if needed, to others—by arguing that what they're doing isn't technically cheating, that it somehow falls short or doesn't qualify.

This kind of legal hairsplitting always has been around, but it was popularized sixteen years ago by Bill Clinton's equivocating during the Monica Lewinsky scandal. Clinton's line, "I did not have sexual relations with that woman," remains the gold standard of the genre, a gem in its combination of outrage, denial, and loophole abuse.

He and Monica, it turned out, were doing a lot of things together that most people would deem adulterous behavior and that the nation later considered inappropriate conduct for the Oval Office. But on technical grounds Bill claimed he wasn't cheating, because having done "it" depends on how you define "it," and in some cases "it" really is "that," but other times it's not.

Many embrace Clinton's legalistic approach, if only in their own minds. They may deem the affair as being acceptable because they flirted but didn't kiss, or kissed but didn't fondle, or fondled but didn't disrobe, or disrobed but didn't have intercourse, or had intercourse but didn't care about it. Each level of behavior can feel to the cheater like it belongs in a different legal category, from misdemeanor to felony to parking ticket. And if you're the only judge and jury for your behavior, this strategy can work really well. If you're not, though, you might want to prepare for cross-examination.

4. CHEATING IS JUST THE SYMPTOM OF A LARGER PROBLEM

PEOPLE WITH BACKGROUNDS in the medical and mental health professions or those with similar sensibilities may be likely to view cheating less through the simplistic lens of right and wrong and more from the complex standpoint of symptoms and root causes. A troubled marriage, in their view, may be the root cause, whereas the cheating is just superficial, merely the most visible manifestation of a deeper problem. The infidelity will have to be dealt with as part of a more comprehensive approach, just as a heroin addict might be given methadone as one element of a recovery program, but neither the cheating nor the heroin is where we should devote the lion's share of our attention and resources.

Advocates of this approach tell themselves that when it comes to infidelity you miss the forest for the trees if you dwell on the affair, so let's not dwell on it. Yes, the cheating was bad and hurtful and indefensible (if also really enjoyable at times), but blaming and shaming are not the answer. After all, the cheater is a victim, too—not a victim of cheating, but a victim of whatever dysfunction or shortcoming led him or her to want to have an affair in the first place. So how about a little compassion?

5. CHEATING AS PAYBACK

I'VE HEARD FROM a surprising number of people who essentially feel entitled to have an affair because their spouse had one. Their justification is as simple as that: payback. In these relationships, those who are the first to cheat often believe they have to grant their spouse a "free pass" if that person ever decides to explore their feelings for someone else, whether it be a fling with a stranger on a business trip or a longer and more dangerous dalliance. What's more, this pass seems to have no expiration date: I've seen them cashed in nearly two decades later.

The "free pass" system is sometimes verbally agreed to but more typically the pass is not discussed and is merely understood. And occasionally the idea of the free pass arises entirely in the moment, when an opportunity for cheating presents itself and the cheated-upon spouse (who otherwise would have remained faithful) thinks, *Okay, my turn.*

The unsurprising aspect of the payback pass is that marriages often don't survive the cashing in, whenever it happens. The fallout from the first affair was damaging and painful enough, and the payback affair proves to be too much to bear. And the whole expectation of "payback" reveals a marriage that has been carrying too great of an imbalance of guilt and resentment anyway.

6. THE AFFAIR IS ONLY ABOUT SEX, NOT LOVE

SOME PEOPLE VIEW sex as a kind of addictive fix, something they need to relieve the tension so they can get on with their lives. As such, they don't imbue sex of this kind with any greater meaning, so they don't think of the cheating they engage in to get their fix as being consequential either, even if they acknowledge its capacity to harm and undermine their primary relationship. They just feel like it shouldn't have to be thought of as being so threatening to their spouse. It was just about sex. If it were about love, that would be a different matter. But it wasn't!

This kind of infidelity might be better explained through the "what if" scenario that some married couples engage in. The couple wonders what would happen if either of them were to become disabled or sick or addled while the other remained healthy, a caretaker, but one who could no longer have sex with the spouse he or she loved. Would that caretaker spouse be allowed or even encouraged to get his or her sexual needs met elsewhere while remaining in love with and committed to the bedridden or otherwise disabled spouse? Surely the answer, with any generous couple, would be yes. So in this case, you just equate the spouse who no longer *can* have sex with the spouse who no longer *wants to* have it, and isn't it basically the same thing?

This approach assumes that the cheated-upon spouse understands this and cares more about the love than the sex and is willing to overlook the fooling around if the affair can be denigrated as meaningless compared to the real love they have created and built up for all these years. And such a justification, couched as an apology, can deliver an indirect message to the cheated-upon spouse as well: Have more sex with me and I won't have to get that fix elsewhere.

7. THE AFFAIR IS ONLY ABOUT ATTENTION, NOT SEX

TO OTHERS, THE sexual aspect of their affair is practically irrelevant, a tawdry sideshow. What they've really been missing in their committed relationship is attention: someone who looks *at* them and not *past* them, who acts like their opinion matters, and who actually listens and cares.

Sex is fun, sure, but so is riding bikes or going out to the movies or engaging in any of the other activities people do together when all they really want is an excuse to hang out with someone who showers them with attention and affection. Sex may be more complicated than those other activities, but it's not what they went looking for; it just sort of happened because sex can be part of attention.

This approach assumes the cheated-upon spouse also is more bothered by the idea of his or her partner enjoying sex with someone than enjoying that person's company and attention, so the importance of the sex gets downplayed. And as above, such a justification, couched as an apology, can deliver an indirect message to the cheated-upon spouse as well: Pay more attention to me and I won't have to seek it elsewhere (and maybe end up having sex as a result).

8. THE AFFAIR WAS A "WAKE-UP CALL" FOR THE MARRIAGE

MANY OF THE previous justifications point to problems in the marriage that led to the affair. And those problems may be insurmountable, with the affair serving as the "ripping off the Band-Aid" moment, forcing the mismatched and long-suffering spouses apart at last. But infidelity also can become a marriage-ending crisis for couples that aren't mismatched and might be happier staying together, yet they think they have to split up because they can't quite get over the betrayal. They can't envision ever trusting again. It's all just too painful.

The love was great, but that just means the devastation is greater. They told themselves when they were young that they would never allow themselves to be doormats, and that if they ever were cheated on they would leave the marriage. And so they do, sadly.

Once people are actually in this situation, though, many realize they don't have to follow that script if they don't want to. They can stay together despite the damage. They can work harder to make up for what was lacking. They don't have to continue with an imbalance of guilt and resentment, or with an expectation of a "free pass" for the spouse who didn't cheat. They can recommit.

Often that commitment is less a blind commitment to faithfulness, as they'd promised at their wedding, than to a wiser and more mature agreement of future honesty and respect. Meaning: if either spouse feels trapped and can no longer continue, if either feels that happiness cannot be found in this relationship, then they need to speak up about it and figure out what to do, not act secretly on their dissatisfaction or impulses by having an affair. For a great many couples, that kind of recommitment agreement can make a huge difference.

More than two decades ago, when a young woman named Judy was newly married, she had no doubt what she would do if she ever were to catch her husband cheating. One evening she was sitting around the dinner table with her girlfriends, most of them newlyweds like her, and discussing everyone's favorite topic: What would you do if your husband had an affair?

Most were unanimous in their outrage.

One said she'd leave in a minute if her husband ever slept with someone else.

Another announced that she'd never trust her husband again. Every time he went out or went away on a business trip, she would suspect him of having an affair, and she simply couldn't live like that.

When it became Judy's turn to speak, she said, "If it was a one-night stand or an overnight business trip, or a company party where everyone had had too much to drink, I guess I could forgive. But a sustained year of lying, sneaking around, and all the makings of a real affair? I'm sorry. That, I could never condone or forgive."

And then that exact scenario played out in her life. A decade later, her husband confessed to her that he'd been having a year-long affair with a waitress, and when the young woman broke up with him, he was so devastated that he couldn't hide it; he had to tell his wife, in part because he needed to talk to someone about it, and she was the person he felt closest to.

After the shock and pain abated a bit, Judy actually felt sympathy for him. He had betrayed her in the worst way imaginable, enacting the exact nightmare she had spoken about years before. But, as she discovered, you don't really know how you're going to feel or react until you're in the situation.

What's surprising to many is how their daily lives must go on, just as when there has been a death in the family, just as in the wake of most tragedies. You continue driving the carpool. You continue going to work. You empty the dishwasher and walk the dogs. And in these routines can come a comfort, a "one foot in front of the other" solace that gets some people through. What's more, though, is they don't feel like the affair erases the love they had for each other over the years and the life they had built. They often feel like they *should* divorce but don't want to.

And in some cases they can be rewarded with better times if they honor that wish. In Judy's situation, they had two small children to consider, and they didn't want to part rashly in a way they would later regret and that might do great harm to their kids. To help themselves start over in their marriage, they decided to move across the country, which forced them together and also unified the family as they struggled to find their way in a new place.

Over the following decade they got new jobs, raised their children, traveled far and wide around the globe, and found a new love and respect for each other. Eventually, after twenty-two years of marriage, they did divorce and go their separate ways, but with an appreciation for what they'd been able to experience together and give their children for all those years.

9

Loyalty

THE DEVOTION TEST

IF FINDING LOVE INVOLVES TAKING QUIZZES, then keeping love seems to involve taking tests. The biggest of these is the devotion test. Have you taken one?

The devotion test challenges your relationship in a way that goes far beyond overcoming bad behavior or petty squabbling. They're the "in sickness," "for worse," "in bad times," and "for poorer" parts of your vows (remember those?) that sounded so romantic when spoken with a celebratory smile before friends and family.

Typically the test will involve dealing with a spouse's serious or life-threatening health problem, which is why many of us don't face our first real devotion test until late in life. But devotion tests can be doled out to anyone at any time: a cancer diagnosis, a traumatic brain injury, a deep depression, or any number of terrible situations that arise without warning or reason.

The "right" choice in handling the situation is usually obvious, if difficult: you are supposed to stand by the person to whom you're committed and help him or her however you can with everything you've got. This is both what you expect of yourself and what others expect of you. You are not supposed to divorce your wife while she's undergoing radiation and chemotherapy or tell your army husband abroad, via Skype, that the separation is just too hard on your marriage, so you've decided to begin seeing other men.

But not all devotion tests come prepackaged with crisp moral clarity. The most challenging fall into a gray zone where you don't really know what's right, what's best, or how much you can give without losing yourself—and neither do those friends and family who might judge you.

Two stories I'll share fall into this gray zone. These situations may not be common, but that doesn't mean the emotions they stir and the kinds of choices they present aren't universal.

I'll present each story in three stages. First, I'll give you each central question and ask how you'd handle the situation in that person's shoes. Second, I'll add more detail to see if that helps with your hypothetical decision making. Finally, I'll reveal what happened to the couples who confronted these tests in real life.

Kerri's Choice

Kerri was falling in love with a man named Theo who revealed, after several dates, that he was HIV positive. If you were Kerri, would you be open to continuing the relationship after hearing this bombshell?

☐ *Yes*
☐ *No*
☐ *Need more information*

Diane's Choice

Not long after Diane's wedding, her new husband confessed to her that he felt more like a woman than a man and wanted to head down the road of transitioning from one sex to the other. If you were Diane, would you be open to remaining married through his transition and beyond if that's what he (soon to be she) wanted?

☐ *Yes*
☐ *No*
☐ *Need more information*

If you answered in each case that you need more information, great job! By showing that you understand love is in the details, not the generalities, you just passed your first hypothetical devotion test. Now let me put some real-life meat on these bones and see if that changes anything.

Kerri's Considerations

When Kerri met Theo, she was nineteen and he was forty-two. (A twenty-three-year age gap? That's even worse!) Divorced, with a teenage daughter, he also was a recovering alcoholic and drug user (Oh, come on!) who had contracted the virus twelve years earlier from sharing a needle with a friend who subsequently died of AIDS. When doctors delivered the bad news to Theo that he was infected—which took place several years before he and Kerri met—they gave him "zero" chance of long-term survival. (Okay, I think we've heard enough details here.)

But wait—Theo's wild behavior took place more than a decade earlier. When Kerri met him, he radiated health and happiness. He showed no signs of the disease and had no damage to his immune system. He was attending AA meetings regularly and taking incredibly good care of himself. His virus was being managed through a cocktail of prescription drugs that allowed him to live a normal life.

Theo's teenage daughter was doing well and lived with her mother. An aspiring landscape architect, Theo was smart, talented, magnetic, and attractive to Kerri in every way.

Now what do you say? If you were in Kerri's shoes, would you be open to continuing the relationship and possibly even getting married?

- ☐ *Continue relationship*
- ☐ *Bail*
- ☐ *Still don't know enough to decide. How did it work out for them in the end?*

Diane's Considerations

When Diane met her future husband they were both in their early forties. This would be a first marriage for both, and neither had children from previous relationships. He actually had confessed to his sexual confusion back when they were dating, saying he'd long been ambivalent about his maleness but had made peace with it. Diane always had found overtly masculine men to be off-putting anyway, and she was drawn to his slender build, blue eyes, intelligence, and compassion.

After they married and he told her of his wish and intention to transition from male to female, Diane was upset but also thought about it in practical terms. She had lived with a female lover in her early twenties, so living in a lesbian relationship again would be agreeable enough to her, though she worried she would miss the societal ease afforded to straight couples, which she would lose in this case.

What's more, she didn't blame him for pulling a bait and switch by saying prior to their marriage that he'd made peace with his maleness, partly because she didn't think he had a deceitful bone in his body, but also because, as he explained to her, it was (ironically) the security of the love and trust he'd found with her that allowed him to admit to himself that he was transsexual and needed to find a way to be his true self. In other words, he didn't have the courage to face the truth about his identity until he felt as fully loved as he did with her.

The hormone treatments and eventual surgery, over many months, would change his face and chest and alter his anatomy, but his essence would remain the same, or so Diane assumed. Would the person she fell in love with still be there? He said he would be. Despite the disruption and difficulty of his coming transition, he promised he would continue to love her after he became a she, or at least wanted to try. Would she try, too?

If you were Diane, what would you say? Do you think you would be able to give him that chance and stay married?

☐ *Yes, stay married and remain open*
☐ *File for divorce*
☐ *Still don't know enough to decide. How did it work out
   for them in the end?*

If you said you still don't know enough to decide, good for you. Because the truth about such tests is that until we're in the situation ourselves—holding hands with our HIV-positive lover in the car, facing our transsexual spouse across the table, or dealing with whatever curveball life has thrown our way—we can't know how we're going to feel. That's the great thing about love; it's never distant and hypothetical but always immediate and personal. And when we try to guess what we'd do based on hypothetical questions, we often underestimate our capacity to be able to adapt, to grow, and to love. We think: *I could never do that.* But when we find ourselves in the situation, we seem to find a way to do it. We're stronger than we thought we were. Or perhaps we're more attached than we ever imagined we could be.

As for how these real-life stories worked out for the couples in the end . . . that, I can answer.

Kerri's Decision

When Kerri and Theo first met she had to admit that he was, on paper, "the worst boyfriend possible." Her mother, big surprise, thought he was the worst boyfriend possible, too. She was so consumed by worry over the man her daughter had chosen that she couldn't sleep at night and even considered threatening to write Kerri out of her will if she continued to see him. "Can't you just find another guy?" she'd ask in exasperation. "Any other guy?"

But Kerri didn't want to find any other guy. She wanted this guy. So despite his HIV-positive status, she stayed with him. They practiced safe sex while trying to be creative. Their bond grew stronger until, six years after meeting, they decided to marry. That was more than two decades ago.

Over the years they have been dealt crushing blows, most painfully the death of Theo's daughter (a woman who by then had two young children of her own), at thirty, to leukemia. But Kerri and Theo have had a full, loving life together. Kerri has never become HIV positive. And Kerri's mother long ago came to love and respect the man she had once feared and urged her daughter to leave.

In an odd twist of fate, however, this brave and committed woman who, on a leap of faith, decided to marry a man who had been given an early death sentence (and just feeling grateful for whatever time they'd get together before he died) was diagnosed a few years ago, at age thirty-seven, with stage-3 breast cancer.

The cancer was an especially aggressive kind that already had spread to her lymph nodes, and her future would involve hospital stays, treatments, insurance nightmares, and bedside vigils—all those routines she'd expected would befall them one day if she were to stay with Theo, but with *him* as the patient and her as the caretaker. Instead it was Kerri confronting her mortality and Theo—her fifty-nine-year-old, HIV-positive husband— taking care of her with love, affection, and hope.

Diane's Decision

Diane wanted to try to see it through with her husband, but she was on edge the day she drove him to the hospital for his facial feminization surgeries, in which the surgeon would carve out more womanly versions of his features: higher eyebrows, a smaller nose, and a more pronounced chin.

Estrogen had already begun to change his look, narrowing and softening his face. But this was really the defining day, for Diane, in terms of starting to think of him as a woman. Although their therapist had for months been urging her to begin using female pronouns for her husband, she just couldn't do it yet. That morning, though, Diane would enter the hospital using words like "husband," "he," and "him," and she'd leave that afternoon saying "wife," "she," and "her."

As they drove to the hospital, though, Diane felt tense and resentful, and she snapped at him for having had a glass of water before they left the house; he'd been instructed not to have any food or drink before surgery.

He was already feeling sheepish and apologetic, repeatedly saying he was sorry, and he felt guilty about what his choice would mean for her. When Diane broke down briefly before he was to be wheeled off to surgery, he said, "I'm sorry for all the pain I'm causing you."

She held his hand, weeping.

"I know why I'm doing this," he said. "But it's just crazy, isn't it?"

She reassured him of the rightness of his decision, telling him to try to focus on the courage he was demonstrating by doing it at all.

And off he went.

Hours later, he was wheeled back as a she, as a wife, or at least that's how Diane viewed this first round of surgery. Once home, she helped "her" inside, made "her" comfortable, turned up the heat. At one point she imagined what her life would be like if her spouse didn't exist. *Easier*, she thought, *but empty*.

She would need to call herself by a new name. Documents and licenses would have to be changed to that name, with all the hassle and awkward questions that process would entail. Months later, more surgery would be required to shave down her Adam's apple and give her breast implants. Genital surgery would follow, along with the other adjustments in transitioning from a straight relationship to a gay one.

All in all, it has been a multiyear devotion test they have passed with flying (rainbow) colors. And today, years later, they remain very much together and in love.

DEVOTION TEST NOSTALGIA

WHEN PEOPLE ARE facing a difficult choice or a health crisis, they understandably want to get through the period of doubt and worry as soon as possible. They yearn for their lives to return to normal, for the dark clouds to pass, and for a happy and healthy ending to their troubles. But once they emerge into that more stable future, they often look back upon their devotion test with surprising feelings of warmth and even nostalgia.

Mark faced his devotion test early in life. He and his wife, Giulia, were only twenty-seven and had been married for just three years when she suffered a psychotic break, fell into a deep depression, and had to be heavily medicated in a way that dulled her personality to a disconcerting state of mostly mute compliance. During this time the normal rhythms of their lives slowed to a crawl as Giulia was too sedated to do much more than plod through her days, and Mark had to scale back his normal schedule so he could devote his time and energy to caring for her.

Though the meds were supposed to modulate the highs and lows Giulia had been experiencing, she would still sink while on them and would speak frequently of suicide when she did, posing questions to Mark such as, "If someone kills herself, does she still get a funeral?"

And he would tell her that she didn't have to think about that, because she wasn't going to kill herself.

"Maybe," she'd say.

"No 'maybe' about it."

"We'll see."

Usually when she talked this way she did so with a sweet smile that reminded Mark of the anticipatory look of pleasure on the face of a child who had been promised ice cream. Given what she was contemplating, however, that anticipatory look of pleasure freaked him out.

Mark's only way to combat Giulia's dreamy talk of suicide during these episodes was to hold her and look into her eyes and remind her how much he and others loved her. Sometimes these conversations about love and death would last for hours. When Giulia was feeling better, she would express how grateful she was to Mark, telling him over and over how wonderful he was, how much he meant to her, and how he was saving her life.

Eventually, with help, the old Giulia emerged; she was able to stop taking the medication, and their lives returned to normal. Yet, happy as they were to come out the other end, intact and seemingly healthy, Mark sometimes couldn't help but notice how trivial and superficial much of their day-to-day interactions now felt compared to the way they'd been during her illness.

That dark period had been terrifying, but the depth of their connection during that phase in their lives, as Mark tried everything he could think of to maintain her spirits and keep her alive, was also, in retrospect, romantic and exhilarating. All they'd ever talked about in those days was love and life and how much they meant to each other; whereas now, like any busy couple with jobs and bills and no time to spare, much of their conversation involved bickering over household chores.

One of them would say, "I cooked dinner, so can you wash the dishes?"

And the other would respond, "Well, I did the laundry today and folded it and put it away, so no."

Feeling nostalgic about closeness forged during difficult times is a relatively common occurrence, if the hundreds of stories I've seen about it are any indication. No one wants to relive the emotional trauma of a frightening diagnosis and treatment or the physical torture of a body-shattering accident. But many of those who have endured times of crisis would like to be able to recapture the feelings of connection, appreciation, and caretaking that bloomed in the midst of their misfortune. They believe that joint struggle brought out their best selves, and they'd like to find a way to access those best selves again. But you can't fake a devotion test, even if you want to. And with bills to pay and deadlines looming, you probably don't have the time to try anyway.

HERE IS WHAT YOU ASK

IT'S OFTEN SAID that we can't always control what happens to us but we can control how we respond. And how we respond can reveal who we are and what we care most about. With that in mind, let's take a look at one final devotion test.

Say your spouse is in a terrible car accident. You get a call from the hospital; the doctor who is tending to your spouse is on the line. Your spouse will survive but is seriously injured. You can ask one question about his or her condition. What would that question be?

This story is about Layng Martine Jr. (pronounced "Lang"), a Grammy-nominated singer and songwriter who lives in Nashville with his wife, Linda. Maybe you have heard songs Layng has written over the last few decades for Reba McEntire, Trisha Yearwood, Jerry Lee Lewis, and even Elvis. Maybe you have heard the number-one country song he wrote for Billy "Crash" Craddock, "Rub It In," which became an ad jingle for Johnson & Johnson's Glade PlugIn air freshener product ("Plug it in, plug it in . . ."). Probably you have heard his music and not known it.

Successful both in career and family, Layng has been married to Linda for more than forty years. They have three children, all boys, who are now grown. Though Layng and Linda live in Tennessee, they have had a house on the Rhode Island coast for decades where they go every summer, just as they've done since their boys were small.

Twenty years ago, when their youngest son was fifteen, they were making their annual trek to the Rhode Island house in two cars. Linda and their son were in one car, and Layng was alone in the other. But shortly into the trip, something went wrong with the car Layng was driving, and they had to pull off the highway in Knoxville to have it checked out at a service station.

Once it became clear the repair wouldn't take too long, Linda suggested she and their son continue on their way. Layng would meet up with them later at a hotel in Allentown, Pennsylvania.

As Linda walked away, Layng thought she looked so pretty in her blue-and-white seersucker dress. He remembered that parting moment well because it would turn out to be the last time he would see her walk. As Linda pulled away, she called out, "See you in a few hours!" and blew him a kiss.

Later that evening, after nightfall, when Layng came upon the traffic jam on the interstate, he felt mostly irritated. He was already exhausted after driving all day, and the backup looked endless, with traffic stopped in both directions. Nobody was moving except for the cars edging along the shoulder toward the exit, with people deciding to try their luck on the back roads.

So that's what Layng decided to try, too. Moving more quickly along the frontage road, he soon saw the cause of the jam, the blinking blue lights of emergency vehicles, an accident, a scene of mangled metal. As he drove past, he couldn't have been much more than a hundred feet away. And all he could think was how glad he was that Linda and their son hadn't gotten stuck in this, that they'd left the repair shop well before him and were way ahead.

Later, he decided to pull off at a diner and call the hotel from a pay phone to let them know where he was and how late he'd be. But when he asked the desk clerk to be connected to the Martine's room, the clerk said there was someone on the other line calling for that room, too, someone from a hospital in Hershey.

His face hot, Layng asked for that number and dialed it. Soon he was on the line with the hospital chaplain, who told him his wife and son were both there, that they had been involved in an accident on the interstate. It was, of course, the accident he had driven right past.

When Layng asked if they were all right, the chaplain put the doctor on.

"Your son is okay," the doctor said. Linda, however, was not okay. She was in very bad shape.

Later Layng would learn that Linda's legs didn't move. He would learn that her legs never would move again. He would sit at Linda's bedside, squeezing her hand, as she would say, with tears in her eyes, "It all was too perfect, wasn't it?"

And Layng would agree that it was too perfect. It always had seemed that way to him, too.

Now, though, on the phone with the doctor, Layng's mind was ablaze with a fear of the unknown. He had no idea of the extent of his wife's injuries; he just knew it was bad. What would their future be? Would it be possible to have any semblance of the relationship and family life they'd had previously?

If you are devoted to your spouse and are unlucky enough to find yourself in this situation, here is what you might ask the doctor. You might think about what is most important to you in your relationship, what's at the heart of your love, and ask, as Layng did, "Can she think?"

"Yes," the doctor said. "Her brain is fine."

And that's when Layng knew they could handle it, whatever "it" would prove to be. No matter how injured Linda was, and no matter how complicated her recovery and future, he knew that if her brain was okay, she would still be the person he loved, the woman to whom he was devoted. As long as her brain was okay, he thought, they would be okay. And they were.

More than okay. They have thrived, with Linda rolling through three full-length marathons, up and down the hills of Tuscany, into pubs in Ireland, and all around Paris, Rome, San Francisco, and Miami, not to mention to Red Sox games at Fenway Park. Layng even got Linda a floatable lawn-chair contraption with wide, inflated tires that allows her to maneuver on the sand, enter the water, and drift in her beloved ocean waves.

They learned that great loss didn't mean they still couldn't have a great life. More to the point, they learned that in their case it was within their power to make their life great if they chose to, so they did. "We wanted it so badly," explained Layng, "and we love it so much."

10

Wisdom

WHEN LOVE IS LIKE E.T.

MY FINAL QUIZ QUESTION AT THE start of this book asked whether you consider love to be primarily a feeling or a choice. Like nearly all of the questions in the starter quiz, I asked partly because I didn't know the answer. And now, ten chapters later, I still don't know whether I consider love to be primarily a feeling or a choice, except to say: "It depends."

So I asked Cathi.

"Romantic love is a feeling," she said without missing a beat. "And married love is a choice."

Gee, thanks.

"Well, actually," she added, backpedaling, "it depends."

"On what?"

That launched us into a spirited debate about feeling love versus choosing it—and we were still discussing this a half hour later. Our conversation even drew in other people at one point when Cathi posed my question to a clump of shoppers in a store we'd wandered into ("He's writing a book about love and wants to know . . ."), prompting total strangers to throw in their two cents as well, much to my mortification.

Alas, our conversation was apparently so forgettable that I forgot it. Which is the whole problem with that question. It *seems* like a great question, and you end up talking about it a lot, but everything you or anyone else says will sound so obvious. Actually, that's not entirely true. Listening to someone drone on about how love is a feeling sounds obvious. Hearing someone explain how or why love is a choice can be complicated and inspiring.

In any event, I felt like I needed to cast a wider net than my wife (smart as she is) and random shoppers (well-meaning as they may have been). So I began to conduct research on the topic. I read articles. I read entire (pages of) books. I looked up stuff online. I scrolled through forums containing years' worth of entries that were, believe it or not, solely devoted to that one question: Is love more of a feeling or a choice?

"it's a chemical reaction in the brain," explained princess_jasmine on one such forum, "that over time creates a bond to the subject in question with the principle [*sic*] point being to produce offspring to keep the species going."

Ah, I see.

"meeting someone is a choice," chirped rim68. "getting to know them better is called interest. wanting to be with them is a feeling called love."

To which barbiedollgirl interjected: "u r comparing apples to oranges."

"both of those work on the right woman," quipped rim68 nonsensically.

Finally, someone named mirr0rmirr0r entered the fray with her emoticon-laced version of the truth: "☺Love is a feeling but you can make choices about your feelings.☺"

"This I agree with," confirmed fun2bchattin.

Would that settle the matter? No.

"I choose all of my feelings," piped up icuddle. "I can turn them on, or off, at will . . . like flipping a light switch. That spooks the hell out of people who witness it."

"We choose who we love," suggested gjlover. "We do not choose who gives us pheromone-induced euphoria. The trick is to figure out which is which."

WHAT GJLOVER MEANS, IN PLAIN ENGLISH, is not unlike what Cathi was saying: we choose the people we love but not those we lust for.

Figuring out which is which, though, doesn't seem to be a problem for anyone I hear from. They know the difference between those they love and those they lust for. What they struggle with is finding someone they both love *and* lust for and having that person feel the same way about them. Because some people simply don't feel lust for the person they love, or they do feel lust for someone they know they'll never love, and they can't understand why.

But getting back to gjlover's point: it seems that what gj calls "pheromone-induced euphoria" (aka pheromone-induced lust) actually applies to animal attraction more than human attraction. In certain animals, especially rodents, males are driven into lust-fueled frenzies when they sense the presence of chemical secretions in a female's sweat and urine. Female dogs in heat, for example, advertise their reproductive readiness through the release of powerful scent markers, and soon the male dogs come running.

That human males might also have this impulse sounds plausible enough (in the sense that any strange behavior involving human males and lust sounds plausible), but scientists maintain that's not how it works with us. Men are not driven into lust-fueled frenzies by detecting the existence of pheromones in a woman's sweat or urine. Though women might have trace amounts of pheromones in their sweat, those traces aren't powerful enough to be the key ingredient in some future love potion. And the smell of a woman's urine won't drive men crazy with desire at all, not even if the woman has just eaten asparagus, which apparently can act as an aphrodisiac (but for its concentration of vitamins and folate, not for how it makes urine smell).

Maybe, researchers wondered, men are the ones who give off pheromones that drive women crazy with desire? To find out, they conducted experiments in which they presented women with a pungent array of men's sweaty, unwashed T-shirts to bury their noses in. And in two such studies, they found that if the women were drawn to any armpit stench at all, it was likely to be a stench that either reminded them of their fathers (how sweet!) or happened to be from a man who had a complementary immune system to the woman's (which boded well for her future offspring's health).

Evidently, this is where our search for the truth has brought us. In trying to unlock the secrets of love and desire, we have

reached the point where we are investigating the erotic implications of asparagus, urine, and armpit stench. Clearly we intend
to leave no stone unturned in this effort. And we have turned
over so many stones already.

You might think, as I sometimes do, that maybe we ought
to just leave love alone. Focus our efforts on loving well and
being kind rather than on smelling dirty laundry in a lab and
recording our stench preferences. But we can't leave love alone,
because, as with everything, we want to get better at it.

Getting better at things is what we human beings strive to
do. Some might say it's what separates us from animals. Emperor
penguins, for example—as much as we may admire them—just
keep sitting on their eggs in the fierce wind and bitter cold year
after year, as they presumably have done as long as penguins
have toddled the earth. If human beings were expected to repro-
duce that way, and we fathers were told to sit on an egg for two
months under those conditions, you can bet that in five minutes
we'd figure out exactly what temperature our egg needed to be
and how much shelter from the wind it required, and in no time
we would invent an EggMate® to do the sitting on our behalf,
freeing us to head over to the South Pole Bar & Grille for some
warmth and beer and female companionship.

We humans, in fact, hardly see anything in our lives that
can't be improved with a little elbow grease and ingenuity. We
push to make progress on all fronts. Even love, we think, can
surely be done better. Just tell us what we need to do to whip
this love beast into shape once and for all, and we'll get to work
and make it happen.

Yet despite all the money, research, electronic innovation,
mathematical wizardry, and decades of experimentation, we

seem to be stuck in neutral when it comes to improving love, still plagued by the same doubts and dilemmas that Shakespeare wrestled with nearly five hundred years ago. What do we know about love that he didn't? What have we learned? What significant breakthroughs make love easier and better now than before? Any?

I can think of exactly one. We seem to have gotten better over time at opening up the castle gates to usher in more kinds of love, which is no small achievement. We appear to be learning, slowly but surely, that love can come in many different packages and arrangements and still be the same thing—no better, no worse. We have improved, as a society, at being able to cheer rather than fear untraditional love of whatever kind, whether the supposed taboo has involved race, class, religion, sexual orientation, physical disability, or mental impairment. Many will still attempt to ban, shame, and demonize love they don't find palatable, but the momentum of public opinion is unlikely to reverse itself. We're learning. We're even becoming more loving, you might say. Or at least more compassionate and understanding.

Meanwhile, the search for wisdom goes on. And I can't help but feel a kinship with those who spend their days tackling the difficult questions of human attraction and attachment, whatever their motivation. Whether you're a scientist investigating the chemicals of lust, a mathematician devising matchmaking algorithms, a jilted lover attempting to come to terms with how your last relationship unraveled, or a writer like me trying to make sense of it all, you've got my deepest sympathies. It's a frustrating and often fruitless task we have taken on, and we're brave to try.

By the same token, though, I have to admit I feel a little sorry for love, too, for being so constantly subjected to our withering scrutiny. Sometimes I can't help but think of love as a living, breathing creature that we're repeatedly capturing, anesthetizing, and experimenting upon in our eagerness to discover what it's made of, to tame it with our systems and rules, and then to send it back into the wilderness with a GPS-enabled tracking collar in the hope that we'll be able to find it easier next time and understand it better when we do.

Which brings me to my final quiz question: If you had to imagine love as a living, breathing creature, what would you pick? A babyish-looking cupid? A furry animal with a heart-shaped face and pink ears? The Dalai Lama? Or something else altogether?

When I imagine love in creature form, I actually picture it being more like E.T. the extra-terrestrial, Steven Spielberg's adorable space alien from thirty years ago who healed bleeding wounds with his glowing finger and exhorted his youthful guardians to "be good." After all, isn't that what love, at its best, is about—healing wounds and being good? In the movie, however, E.T. is pursued so relentlessly by the scientists and government agents charged with figuring out what the hell this magical creature is, how he works, and where he comes from, that by the end E.T. winds up near death on a makeshift operating table, his red life-light dimming, electrodes taped all over his dehydrated body.

When I consider our increasingly aggressive and well-funded efforts to "decode" and demystify love—and where such efforts might ultimately lead—I can already imagine the scene: those same scientists in their goggles and jumpsuits looking grimly down upon love's cold carcass and muttering, "Well, not much we can do at this point. Too bad we had to kill love to understand it. That's the last thing anyone wanted. But at least now we can perform an autopsy and discover what makes this sucker tick."

Here's the thing: If we happen to be scientists eager to explain love's secrets, we may be drawn to study human attraction and bonding in a laboratory and identify its chemical origins. If we're businesspeople, we'll want to conduct surveys and cull online dating data to improve our clients' matching success, grow our company, and swell our bottom line. If we're authors and newspaper editors, we'll probably be left to search for understanding by reading tens of thousands of strangers' love stories and then writing books of categories and theories and trends. And maybe these efforts will help us decide whom to love, where we might find him or her, and how we can increase our odds for a positive and lasting outcome.

That's all great. I'm not going to argue against the pursuit of knowledge and understanding whatever the subject. But as we poke, prod, analyze, and theorize, let's not get so carried away in our push for answers that we end up with a cold carcass on our hands. Let's try to embrace love's complexities as much as we try to explain them away. And let's make sure we step back every so often, with humility, to marvel at the mystery of what love does best: it helps us to be good.

ACKNOWLEDGMENTS

I OWE SPECIAL THANKS to my agent, Amanda Urban, for suggesting this project years ago and then for checking in, prodding, and sharing her ideas and enthusiasm and belief until I finally understood what was possible and was able to make a go of it.

Cathi Hanauer was indispensable to this effort, as she is with all of my work, and my life. As my best reader and first editor, she isn't shy with her red pen, but she also laughs in all the right places. My love and thanks to you, Cathi, yet again.

Thanks to my longtime editor at William Morrow, Henry Ferris, for taking me on once more, for making my work better and presenting it so well, and for guiding me through the publishing maze with such intelligence, decency, and good humor. At Morrow, I am also grateful for the efforts of Sharyn Rosenblum, Megan Swartz, and Cole Hager.

At the *New York Times*, I owe a huge debt of gratitude to former Style editor Trip Gabriel, as does my entire family. He changed our lives when he dreamed up the Modern Love column nine years ago and invited me on board. And he opened another door when he asked me in January 2006 to report on what I'd learned about love as the column's Valentine's Day offering that year. It was an assignment I then gave myself several more times over the following years, ultimately planting the seeds for this book.

Thanks to current *Times* Style editor, Stuart Emmrich, and his deputy, Laura Marmor, who have been the best bosses and colleagues anyone could imagine. I value their guidance, friendship, ideas, support, and sense of humor more than I can say.

Thanks to my parents, Charles and Vera Jones, to whom this book is dedicated. They have encouraged my creative work all my life, and I'm ever grateful.

Thanks to Lonnie and Bette Hanauer for their love, friendship, and travel opportunities, especially that cruise to Alaska, where I was able to jump-start this book in the ship's lido deck cafeteria while my four-thousand-plus fellow cruisers watched whales spout and glaciers calve. My conversations with Amy Hanauer that week helped a lot, too, as they always do—thanks, Amy. It also was on that trip, apparently, that I began to understand my professional life through cruise-ship metaphors.

Thanks to my children, Phoebe and Nathaniel, who have taught me as much about love as anyone. You two make everything better.

Thanks to the late, great Steve Orlen, former director of the MFA program in creative writing at the University of Arizona, for unwittingly playing Cupid when he added my name to Cathi's lunch list.

Thanks to Kate Christensen and Brendan Fitzgerald for their love, generosity, and culinary skills, and also for that November week of writing solitude on Conway Lake.

Thanks to the Writers' Mill in Florence, Massachusetts—my refuge.

Thanks to Brian Rea, whose evocative and poignant illustrations have graced the column these last several years and whose artwork I'm thrilled to feature on the cover of this book. And my admiration and appreciation to the column's previous illustrators, Christopher Silas Neal and David Chelsea, who brought humor and beauty to the column with their distinctive styles.

Thanks to those friends and relatives who generously listen to me talk about this material year after year and help in ways both obvious and not: Joe B. Jones, Betsy Gorman, Judy Hanauer, Mark Cassell, Dave Spring, Robbie Myers, Frank Michielli, Gina Russell, Margot Guralnick, Chris Russell, Ted Conover, Stan Yarbro, and John Marks.

Finally, thanks to the hundreds of writers I have worked with over the years and the tens of thousands of others who have shared their stories with me. Being immersed in their lives and struggles has been an education and a privilege, and I am grateful to have been trusted with what for many of them is the most important story in their lives.

FURTHER READING

New York Times Modern Love essays referenced in this book include (in order of mention):

"Like New! (With a Few Broken Parts)" by Irene Sherlock, January 23, 2005

"Snappish at First, Now All Warm and Fuzzy" by Candida Pugh, August 14, 2009

"How I Earned My Wings Back" by Tiffany Hawk, January 8, 2010

"Diary of a Soldier's Wife: Tie-Dye and Camo Don't Mix" by Sophia Raday, June 18, 2006

"Stand by Your (Marlboro) Man" by Hyla Sabesin Finn, August 21, 2005

"Looking for Signs That It's Meant to Be" by Liz Falletta, April 12, 2012

"Deep in the Past, a Link to Bind Us" by Patrick Connolly, April 21, 2011

"A World Away, a Wish Answered" by Natalie Appleton, March 2, 2012

"Sometimes, It's Not You" by Sara Eckel, September 23, 2011

"First Comes Marriage" by Farahad Zama, June 5, 2009

"A Leap of Faith" by Renee Watabe, July 3, 2005

"What the Rabbi Said" by Amy Klein, December 17, 2010

"Yes, I Really Am Bisexual. Deal With It" by Wilson Diehl, April 25, 2013

"'Maddy' Just Might Work After All" by Jennifer Finney Boylan, April 24, 2009

"A Kite That Couldn't Be Tied Down" by Lisa Ruth Brunner, July 29, 2010

"Our Joy Knows No Bounds, Or Lanes" by Ellen Graf, December 30, 2007

"My Mr. Right, in the Land of Make-Believe" by Kim Gamble, January 30, 2009

"Ready in Case the Other Shoe Should Drop" by Julia Anne Miller, March 21, 2013

"Even in Real Life, There Were Screens Between Us" by Caitlin Dewey, April 28, 2011

"Do Not Adjust Your Screen or Sound" by Heather Sellers, June 13, 2013

"So Tell Me Everything I Know About You" by Joanna Pearson, September 12, 2008

"Honey, Let's Get a Little Divorced" by Rachel Zucker, December 2, 2010

"An Open and Shut Marriage" by Colette DeDonato, February 3, 2008

"Truly, Madly, Guiltily" by Ayelet Waldman, March 27, 2005

"After the Affair" by Judy Wachs, November 23, 2012

"On the Precipice, Wings Spread" by Kerri Sandberg, August 27, 2010

"My Husband Is Now My Wife" by Diane Daniel, August 18, 2011

"Out of the Darkness" by Mark Lukach, November 25, 2011

"In a Charmed Life, a Road Less Traveled" by Layng Martine Jr., March 6, 2009

DANIEL JONES has edited the Modern Love column in the Sunday Styles section of the *New York Times* since its inception in October 2004. His books include two essay anthologies, *Modern Love* and *The Bastard on the Couch*, and a novel, *After Lucy*, which was a finalist for the Barnes and Noble Discover Award. His writing has appeared in the *New York Times, Elle, Parade, Real Simple,* and *Redbook,* among others. He lives in Northampton, Massachusetts, with his wife, writer Cathi Hanauer, and their two children.